In the Name of Grace

John Calu

For Zully & Vanessa,
with love, respect & admiration

ACKNOWLEDGEMENTS

This book would not have been possible without the research, guidance, love, and support of many wonderful people.

I am deeply thankful for the generosity of Thomas J. Calu, Avah & Al Gallo, Patti Minnick, Dave Hart, Victoria Ford, Vivian Baker, Rob Colding, Bob & Jeanne Stives, Matt, Dina, Adam & Carole Calu, Eric Maywar, Marlena White, Carol South Watt, Joanne Vaccaro Kish, the Marshalls, the Beers, the Schipskes, the Bullocks, the Chorbas, JoAnne Banks, Eugene Guillemette, Anthony & Debbie Genovese, Karl J. Flesch, Laura Poll, Elizabeth Yull, Tom Glover, Sally Lane, Wendy Nardi, Leighanna Shirey, Sparklle Rainne, Sarah Fader and the entire team at Eliezer Tristan Publishing.

CHAPTER ONE

SHE WAS BORN ON HALLOWEEN in 1925, and her entrance into this world was accompanied by a record-breaking snowfall. The Delaware River had already frozen over, and the usually bustling streets of the city were slick, cold, and quiet. The headlines in the *Trenton Evening Times* spoke of a demand made by the League of Nations on France, protests over Syrian bombing, and the arrest of a Negro for drunken driving.

The child was pale, but not frail, with bright blue eyes and raven-colored hair. Martha Knowlton Smyth, or Maddie, as she was known, had carried full-term and was twenty-two years old when she gave birth to Grace. Grace's father, Lloyd Smyth, was only nineteen at the time. They named her after his mother in a transparent plea for her support – and apparently it worked, since they lived under her roof for quite some time. Lloyd stayed out of the way while his mother taught his wife how to run a boarding house, raise a child, hold down a job, and keep track of an immature, potentially wayward young husband and father. She had plenty of experience to draw upon, being prematurely widowed herself.

All Lloyd's father had left them was a pile of bills and a Kodak No. 2 Brownie box camera. He had taken pictures of Times Square in New York City before moving his wife and kids south to Trenton, New Jersey, when he landed a sales job with the prestigious RC Maxwell

Company, famed for outdoor advertising. He would go on to land the account for Liberty Bonds from the U.S. Government and a pilot program with Coca-Cola for billboards on the boardwalk in Atlantic City. John Smyth passed away in 1910, at thirty-five years of age, after nine years of marriage, leaving Grace and their two sons to fend for themselves. His namesake would grow up and leave in his teens for parts south, never to be heard from again. Lloyd would grow up to father his mother's namesake and develop a fondness for the adventures he associated with a father he never really knew.

On the night his daughter was born, Lloyd was having drinks with a childhood friend and passing out cheap cigars at The Tremont House while listening to a piano player and enjoying the company of a few scantily clad flappers all dressed up for a costume party.

"I'm telling you, Danny, if I can get my hands on a Leica 1, they'll never know what hit 'em." Lloyd was cooking up another fool-proof plan to strike it rich, but Danny wasn't buying it. Lloyd couldn't even look him in the eye.

"Lloyd, that camera costs as much as a decent house, and that's what you should be thinking about buying, now that you've got a little one to care for," Danny drained his glass and got up to leave.

"Danny, my friend. That's what the camera is for!" Lloyd almost burst out loud, waving his hands with a flourish like he was on stage. "I'm telling you there's money in advertising, and I've got an eye for what they want."

He put his hands in front of his face and clicked imaginary photos of a flapper's legs, breasts, and face in that order before winking at her and grabbing his buddy by the arm to stop him from leaving.

These two were as thick as thieves. In August 1921, at sixteen years of age, Lloyd and Danny had been arrested for riding bicycles after dark and fined one dollar each. They were inseparable after that, and luckily, Lloyd's mom had a soft spot for her son's pure Irish friend. Where Lloyd was tall and slender, and a little too handsome for his own good, Danny was a bit on the portly side, with thick red hair and freckles, to boot. He kept Lloyd out of trouble as best he could and wished he had half his confidence. When Lloyd tried to order another drink, the bartender shot him down with a piercing glance. There was a prohibition on alcohol, so the Tremont only served "ginger ale" and "sarsaparilla," to which careful barmen could add a touch of whiskey for a dollar when they were sure they weren't being observed. He wasn't taking any chances on Lloyd, who was a little too loud for his own good. It seemed like only yesterday he had turned off Lloyd's father's tab – in the good old days when drinking was still legal – for much the same reason.

"Now don't ye think ye should be home with the missus about now, lad?" the stern older man advised. "I hear they named the little one after yer mother. 'Tis Grace and she is fair of face," he added, smiling as he raised a glass to all who would share his cheer.

Danny tried to stifle a laugh when he heard Maddie had named their daughter for Lloyd's mother. "Serves you right for not being there," he let slip, more out of drunkenness than spite, hoping Lloyd would forgive him for saying so. Lloyd was quick to capitalize on Danny's remark and would make him pay for it, since he was a little low on cash at the moment. He talked Danny into cajoling a celebratory bottle off the bartender for a hefty price. He knew an Italian florist around the corner that started prepping for the weekend late at night, so they banged on the back door long enough to convince him to sell them a nice bouquet of roses. Danny tried to talk him into getting something to eat, but Lloyd was determined to make a grand entrance and needed one more prop. "Something for the baby," he muttered under his breath, rambling on a bit about family and obligations. He could hear his own heartbeat pounding in his ears, but he was sure that he could tough it out if he could just find something for his little girl. Lloyd made Danny drop him off a few blocks away so he could walk off the jitters. His eyes darted from side to side, scouring the neighborhood for whatever he could scavenge.

He arrived home in the wee hours at 437 Walnut Avenue with a dozen roses for his wife, a rare bottle of Bushmills to share with his mother in honor of the ancestors back in Belfast, and a pink crocheted blanket he had pulled off a clothesline two blocks away for his little girl. Some poor woman had left it out to dry and forgotten it. He fluffed it up as best he could and used the ribbon from around the roses to make it look store bought. He may not have been there for her arrival, but he knew how to spin a web of wonder around his daughter's lineage and managed to charm his way out of all but the most egregious offenses. Maddie was a sucker for his *joie de vivre*, and even his mother couldn't resist him when he dreamed out loud, just like his father.

As luck would have it, little Gracie was born on a Friday. That gave her father time to recover from celebrating her birth. Maddie wouldn't be going back to work for a few months after having the baby, but her mother-in-law was a supervisor at the Capital Coat and Apron Supply Company, so her seat in the spooling department would be there when she was ready. The company had just instituted a five-day work week, so Grace the elder had time to attend to her household chores on

Saturday. It was the first of the month, and that meant she would have to make the rounds and collect the rent. She paid thirty-five dollars a month to rent the whole house, and that was a tidy sum to manage, but she collected fifteen dollars from each of her four gentlemen boarders, which allowed her and her son's family to live for free, even if one of her tenants was late to pay, and one of them always was. This time it was Mr. Joseph Woods who came up a little short.

"I'll have it for you next Friday, missus; they're giving me an extra shift at the mill," he pleaded humbly, and she let him off the hook after making him swear to it.

He had steady work at the Roebling plant, and she knew he was good for it. Her son, on the other hand, could never seem to hold down anything remotely steady. He was out late most nights, supposedly selling advertising for the *Trenton Evening Times* – always one sale away from a big score. Whatever money he did make, he blew on the most impractical things he could find. They did have the only Radiola set in the neighborhood, and that must have cost him more than a month's rent, but he said he knew a guy who gave him a great price. He always knew a guy.

They turned off the radio after listening to the *Ever Ready Battery Hour*. Maddie had already gotten the baby to sleep, and her mother-in-law went off to play cards with a neighbor, leaving her alone with Lloyd.

"Lloyd, honey, I know you're just about to land an ad from that banker you were out with the other night, but after that, maybe you could look for something a little steadier?" Maddie came at him gently, in contrast to his mother, hoping to win him over and motivate him at the same time. "You know we can't live rent-free off your mom forever, and the baby's gonna need some things as she grows up," she added cautiously, treating him like the skittish husband he was.

At first, he seemed to take it well. "Listen, Maddie, I'm going to make things good for us." But then, he stood up and started pacing around the room. "The advertising field is just about to explode," he continued, building up steam. "I just heard that Young & Rubicam have outgrown Philadelphia, and they're moving their office to New York! KYW is looking for somebody to sell radio sponsorships now that the tobacco wars are heating up. You know what they say: If Lucky Strike offers fifty bucks for a ten-minute spot, Chesterfield will pay you sixty!" He was pointing at her now, almost accusingly, "I know it sounds like pie in the sky, honey, but I can probably pull down more than a hundred a week once I make a few more connections in Philly and New York." He spoke to her as if she worked in the industry alongside him.

She knew better than to tackle his fantasies head on. She let him finish his sales pitch and sit down beside her before she responded. All she could do was subtly plant a seed every now and then and hope something would eventually grow roots. She knew he was smart. She knew he was lazy. She knew he was a decent guy, and she hoped he would eventually settle down. "I hear Roebling has quite a few openings. Now that they're adding shifts, maybe they could use a bright guy like you?" She snuggled up beside him on the sofa and opened up a copy of *TIME* magazine. Lloyd followed her gaze, then pulled the magazine away from her to look at the cover.

"Can you imagine what they get for a full-page ad? I'll bet Roebling would pay a pretty penny for that if I came up with something clever. If not, there's bound to be some money out of Pittsburgh. Those steel companies are really cooking now. Not to mention all the car companies in Detroit."

Lloyd went on and on, trying to convince himself there were all these amazing potential customers out there looking for an idea man like him. Maddie sighed and slipped off to enjoy a bath before the baby woke up again. She left Lloyd sweating over his financial future and the fortunes of his growing family. He poured himself a shot of Bushmills, remembering he owed Danny ten bucks for the bottle. He started a mental tally of all the IOUs he had left around town and tried to wash them away with another shot.

There were two material things in the Smyth household that Maddie enjoyed to their fullest: The brand new radio in the living room provided her news and entertainment, and the oversized claw-foot tub in the indoor bathroom allowed her an hour of luxurious and total privacy every Saturday evening. Her mother-in-law set the bath schedule, giving Maddie that prime time slot in the hopes that her son would take her out on a Saturday night once in a while, instead of prowling speakeasies and gin joints alone, like his father had so often done to ill effect. There was an outhouse for the gentlemen boarders in case of emergencies, and they knew better than to mess with Mrs. Smyth's schedule.

Maddie stretched her full length in the tub and wondered why all the Knowlton women were so short. Her father had been fairly tall, and both her older brothers, Charles and Joseph, were better than average height, but all seven sisters were a little on the lesser side of that scale. She got sad for a moment, remembering there was an eighth sister, Margaret, who had died at nine years old, before she had a chance to see how tall she could grow. Now, a mother herself, Maddie could only imagine how much that had devastated her poor mom. Annie Knowlton was a gentle but strong woman who raised her daughters well and prided herself on their reputations. Every Knowlton girl knew how to cook and sew. Cleanliness was not only next to godliness, but it was the greatest way to demonstrate your self-respect.

Maddie ruminated as she scrubbed between her toes and looked forward to trying out the cocoa butter her older sister Ruth had given her to ease the stretch marks pregnancy had left behind. Ruth had been so nice to her lately; it was like night and day. She had always fought with her older sister, but now that Maddie was settling into married life and motherhood, Ruth treated her like she treated their mom. Maddie got out of the tub reluctantly when the water had cooled and gently dried herself with the fluffiest towel they had. As she rubbed the cocoa butter on her belly, she was swept up in a wave of sympathy for Ruth, realizing she had attended their mother through each and every one of her many births. Her thoughts gave way to feelings of sadness for her mom. What a difficult life she led, raising so many children, and yet she never complained. Her husband was a good man. Her children were well-behaved and healthy for the most part. They had food on the table, and, although it wasn't much, they made the most of it and enjoyed the simple things in life.

Like most young men of their day, Charles and Joseph had fewer household chores, but their father would have cuffed them good if either one ever disrespected their sisters or their mother. Robert Knowlton was a quiet, hardworking man. His only vices were a little hard cider in the summer and a nice pipe full of cherry tobacco around Christmastime. When he died so suddenly, it was a severe blow to the family.

As Maddie's mother-in-law put it: "You mean to tell me the damned fool gave his life saving somebody else's?"

After narrowly escaping flames, Robert Knowlton had gone back onto the factory floor of the Cook Linoleum Plant when he heard someone screaming behind him. He managed to lift heavy machinery off a pinned-down man to free him but couldn't survive the burns he suffered in the process.

Charles was with the U.S. Cavalry in France at the time, but he came back to help the family as soon as he could. Without their father's income, the family was heading into dire straits, but the Cook Linoleum Company's insurance policy provided them enough money to transition to a smaller home, and they made do with fewer mouths to feed since Joseph and Maddie had already moved out.

When Maddie told her mother-in-law about the insurance company, the elder Grace wanted to know how much they had gotten and why they hadn't hired a lawyer to go after more. She may have had a soft spot for her granddaughter, but the woman was no easy mark for anyone else.

After playing the events of the last year and a half in her mind, Maddie's hour of luxury was nearly over. She turned to a jar of Pond's Vanishing Cream to ease the wrinkles on her brow and remembered her mother telling her not to fret the past. Lloyd had already gone out for the evening before she made it back to the living room, and the baby was crying alone in her crib. She gently picked up little Gracie and cradled her in her arms with all the love and tenderness anyone could ever give, knowing her life would not be easy but that she would do everything she could to make it good.

Surprisingly, the next day, Lloyd joined his wife and mother for the baby's first Sunday church service. Neither the Knowltons nor the Smyths were very religious, but going to church on Sunday was just something everybody did. It was social and respectable – a peaceful way scoundrels could ask forgiveness for whatever they had done on a Saturday night and a way for decent folks to spend a little time together before the work week started over again. Lloyd surprised Maddie again when he invited her mom and sisters to join them all for lunch at the Hildebrecht Restaurant on West State Street. *He must have had one hell of a Saturday night*, his mother thought.

They passed the baby around from sister to sister, little Gracie cooing all the time, and Maddie felt incredible warmth and affection toward Lloyd for making this reunion happen. While some dined on a delicate filet of sole and others a hearty Yankee pot roast with noodles, creamed spinach, mashed potatoes, rolls, butter, and even ice cream for dessert, Lloyd regaled the women with tales of how some friends of his were about to build a ten-story hotel on top of this very restaurant. He, of course, was in on the planning stages and might be willing to accept a position as Vice President of Advertising.

"After all, advertising is the industry that will propel the future," he boasted to a table at which everyone was enjoying the food too much to care about what he said – everyone except Maddie's younger sister Bessie, who seemed to hang on his every word. She even counted the bills he laid out when he paid the check, realizing he had tipped generously on top of the dollar and twenty five cents each person's plate had cost. He noticed her paying attention and rewarded her with a sly little wink as he folded the rest of his bills in a shiny gold money clip. He had had a great night rolling dice behind the Tremont and figured this would buy him some much needed peace on the home front.

Later that night, Maddie thought it was really sweet of him to suggest they give the baby a middle name from someone in her family, to distinguish from his mom's name. She was happy he had hit it off with the Knowlton family and was thrilled he was doing well enough in advertising to treat them to such a special luncheon. When he suggested Bessie for the baby's middle name, she thought it was perfect.

Over the next couple of years, there were no major events in their lives. There was a slow, steady increase in the distance between husband and wife, noticeable in how infrequently they spent a Saturday night or Sunday morning together. The baby grew and learned to crawl. Maddie left her with a variety of babysitters in the neighborhood and went back to work at the Capital Coat and Apron Company. She enjoyed it even though the spooling process was repetitive and physically demanding. Her arms got stronger and her back ached a little bit, but the lunch room camaraderie with the other girls made up for it, since she didn't have a lot of time to spend with her sisters these days, and she was tired of talking with the men in her house. Their favorite topic of conversation was to wonder where her husband was most nights.

Lloyd was getting thinner, and he constantly fretted over improving his wardrobe. He had bought himself a couple of nice suits from Wanamaker's Department Store in Philadelphia. He had to go back a couple times for fittings and wished he could have afforded an apartment there. The train was quick from Trenton, but he liked the action the bigger city afforded a mover and shaker like himself. Trenton was getting small for him. He was doing well enough as an independent advertising salesman for newspapers and radio stations to put away a tidy little nest egg that his wife and mother knew nothing about. He was thinking about getting him and Maddie their own house, but he wanted something big over in Cadwalader Park, where the real money people in Trenton lived. That would show those bastards who didn't think he was good enough. Most of his clients were conservative people from good families with old money and boardrooms in their bloodlines. They had very little experience when it came to advertising and considered it a necessary evil – at best, an entertainment. He treated them to a good night out, including booze and dancing girls, both of which he knew where to find. He could show them the five-star treatment because he knew how to tip the help. The next day, he would visit them in their offices and lock them into a yearlong ad campaign, implying he would keep the previous night secret from their families and less adventurous associates. He was starting to get good at it, but he was never one to be easily satisfied. He wanted in with the Rockefellers, the Fords, the Dukes, and the DuPonts – those people whose money made money for them. No one could accuse him of thinking small.

In the summer of 1928, Lloyd accepted an invitation from a friendly Philadelphia shop girl to spend the weekend in Atlantic City. She was easy on the eyes, but he was more excited about the chance to hobnob with some real money men like the guys who ran the Atlantic City casinos and maybe even make a bootleg connection to further his business. He told his wife he was heading to Scranton, Pennsylvania, for an advertising convention. She had gotten so used to his coming and going as he pleased that it didn't faze her. As long as he handed a little money over at the end of every month, neither his wife nor his mother complained anymore.

After a long night of guzzling top-shelf booze and skinny dipping with a couple of willing companions, Lloyd woke up on the beach, hungover, wearing nothing but a t-shirt and his best pair of trousers, with his shirt, wallet, jacket and shoes missing. He sat there with his head in his hands, watching the sunrise, entirely alone in the world, and cried for all he was worth. The great man about town was no match for a cute little hustler, let alone any Atlantic City gangsters he never got close enough to meet. His whole body trembled even though the sun was warm and the day was bright. He took a few tentative steps before falling back on a sand dune. He covered his head with his t-shirt and screamed with all his might until anger replaced his embarrassment. He slowly made his way back to the boardwalk and bummed a dime off a doorman he had tipped the night before so he could call his old buddy, Danny, who came to his rescue, no questions asked.

"What the hell is it with you, Lloyd? You've got a good gal at home. You're making some decent money. You've got a beautiful baby daughter. And all you want to do is go whoring around! I thought you were a better man than that!" Danny spoke his mind on the ride back to Trenton, thinking maybe he could finally reach his friend now that he had hit bottom.

"I'm just looking to get more out of this miserable life than my old man did," Lloyd snapped back at him defensively. He went on to vent about how bad the poor people have it while the rich people drink champagne and drive German sedans. He compared his lot in life to the guys making money on their investments and always came up short. When Danny dropped Lloyd off at home, he realized it would be the last time he saw him. If Lloyd couldn't appreciate what he had by now, Danny knew he never would.

As summer turned to fall and then winter, little Gracie took over the house. At three years old, she could jabber with the best of them and made it her mission to visit everyone in the household throughout the day. Lloyd seemed like the only one around who was immune to her charms, even though he was spending more evenings at home than he used to. His self-image had been shattered by the weekend he spent in Atlantic City, but he found no solace in the comforts of home. As they listened to the radio, Gracie would dance to Guy Lombardo and the Canadians. She would sing along to "I Can't Give You Anything but Love, Baby!" Everybody in the house would smile and clap for her. They would all quiet down for the news hour, and the star of the house would fall asleep before it was over. Lloyd would drink himself to sleep much later, muttering that he was nothing like his old man, no matter what his mother said.

Amelia Earhart became the first woman to fly solo across the Atlantic in 1928. Herbert Hoover won the presidency over Al Smith by a landslide and was sworn in on March 4. Ironically, sharing the official start of the Great Depression on October 29, 1929, the city of Trenton celebrated Education Day and its two hundred and fiftieth birthday with exhibitions at the armory and a huge parade through downtown. It was so close to Halloween that some kids were wearing costumes. A soon-to-be-four-year-old Gracie was one of them, and she enjoyed the celebration as if it were her own.

Maddie dragged her mother-in-law with them to see the parade, and they ran into the rest of the Knowlton family once they got to the corner of Market and Broad Streets. An old woman made her way through the crowd with a basket full of kittens and handed a solid black one to little Gracie. Her grandmother snatched it out of her hands and tossed it back in the basket, cursing at the old woman before she could get away. She didn't need another mouth to feed. Unfortunately, one tiny little claw had dug into the baby's finger before she could let go, and both Graces ended up screaming at the same time.

Finally alone in his mother's boarding house, Lloyd had reached the end of his rope. His job was going nowhere. He was never going to be rich. Even though he had stopped his gambling and womanizing, nothing made him happy anymore. He couldn't sleep. He couldn't eat. He just sat there in the living room, rocking back and forth, unable to calm himself down. After almost three years of careful saving, he had lost every dime he had to the whims of the stock market on a tip from some broker, even though he knew deep down the whole thing was rigged by the guys who had already made their money. He was sure Maddie and little Grace would be better off without him. He kneeled down next to the stove, turned on the gas jets in the oven without lighting them, and stuck his head inside.

Thankfully, two of the gentlemen boarders, both good Irishmen and fond of their landlady, found Lloyd's body before the family came home from the parade. It would be years before Grace knew how her father had died. Her fourth birthday passed with no further celebration.

CHAPTER TWO

AS TRENTON AND THE REST of the nation slipped into the Great Depression, Maddie slid into one of her own. Rumors of her husband's infidelities had not followed him into the grave, and she sensed people's cruel pity when she passed them on the street. If not for the support of her mother-in-law, whose seniority saved a spot for her to spool on the few shifts left running at the plant, she surely would have been destitute.

Her arms ached from forcing the wheels and gears to grind forward until the loud and noxious generators kicked in. She breathed in oily fumes caught in a poorly ventilated shop all day and stifled her coughs at night to keep the baby from waking up. While the elder Grace ran card games on the weekends and charged the players for bootleg gin, Maddie started quilting with her sisters to sell to those few people unaffected by the financial ruins all around them.

Only two of the four boarders had managed to hold on to any work. The other two hopped a train to New York, thinking they might have better luck there. They never did return. Grace started renting out the other rooms by the week, collecting whatever she could get and cramming whole families into single rooms when they had nowhere else to go. The house took on an air of constant illness, and, even though Maddie did her best to scrub the place from top to bottom every Sunday, by midweek it was almost as hard to endure as the unhealthy workplace she came home from.

The winter of 1929 watched as Trenton deteriorated. One after another, stores and factories closed and families headed west or south for a warmer climate with all of their belongings, hoping against hope that there were jobs to be found. The exodus did not relieve the burden of those it left behind. There was still only work for one of every six or seven able-bodied men or women. Everyone hoped the spring would bring about new jobs in construction. They didn't realize the full extent of the financial crash.

In early March, the ever-resourceful Grace came by some young tomato plants and squash seeds. She enlisted her granddaughter's help in planting a victory garden in an effort to teach the girl something useful and to give Maddie some much needed rest. In truth, Grace needed her daughter-in-law and granddaughter as much as they needed her, though she never admitted that to anyone.

Maddie was nearly broken. She suffered bouts of bursitis in her right arm almost every night, and the morning light stabbed her in the forehead, forcing her to shut the curtains and pray the day would go away. She had used up all her tears and just stared blindly now, no room left for thought, numb to any feeling.

Even though her sisters had problems of their own, they forged a plan to drag Maddie out of her doldrums as soon as the weather permitted them a day at the beach. The thought of that alone gave her something to hold onto through a season that was otherwise hopeless.

Little Gracie learned to leave her mother alone and quietly moved about the house, finding corners she could hide in to look at the picture books that were her only companions. Every time her grandmother found her, there was cleaning to do or something to carry somewhere. The only time she went out was to stand silently alongside her mother in a long line to get some bread.

In the summer of 1930, Ray Davidson was living with his big sister, Annie Knowlton, to help out her and the family with rent and groceries. He was one of the lucky ones who managed to hold a steady job, due in no small part to a friendly disposition and a tireless work ethic. At 21 years of age, he made the grave mistake of buying a car that was almost big enough for the entire family. His weekends that summer were never his own. The Knowlton girls had their young uncle wrapped around their fingers. Money was tight, but he made enough to put gas in the car, and they knew how to pack a picnic lunch for day trips to the Jersey Shore. July 4th fell on a Friday that year, so little Gracie celebrated Independence Day with her first of many trips to Seaside Heights.

Maddie had tried to get out of going, but her kid sister Bessie wouldn't let her. "There is no way in hell I'm watching all these brats myself!" Bessie exclaimed with mock irritation, pointing to five-year-old Gracie. In truth, they had brought along Ray's fifteen-year-old cousin, Marion, to watch Gracie and give Maddie a break. Rounding out the party was their younger sister, Hazel, who had just turned 18. She told Gracie she was named after the color of her eyes, and Gracie got confused because hers were the same. "Is my real name, Hazel, too?"

The drive from Trenton took a little over an hour. The pine forests on the way were so green and pleasant that everyone but Maddie breathed them in deeply and enjoyed the scenery. She couldn't shake a feeling of doom but did all she could to put up a good front. She was ashamed of herself for not being able to show appreciation for her family's efforts to cheer her up. She knew they had it just as hard as she did.

Ruth had stayed home to help their mom out with the endless chores around the house. Lily had married and moved out the year before, leaving two little girls behind for her mother and older sister to raise when she couldn't afford to care for them herself. No one had heard from her since. Carrie had also gotten married recently and was starting a family with a fine young man named Jacob Beers, whom she had met when they both worked at Belle Mead Sweets, a candy factory in Trenton. The youngest sister, Myrtle, wasn't feeling well that day or she would have squeezed into the Ford wagon, too.

Ray Davidson's smile was infectious. Gracie caught a glimpse of it from the back seat, dazzling her in the rear view mirror. She snuggled up between Marion and Hazel, feeling warmth from head to toe. Bessie went on about some guy she had met, then whispered with crude implication to a truly disinterested Maddie that he might be "worth a tumble."

They made it to the shore and found a place to park the car two blocks away from the boardwalk on Franklin Street. They grabbed a big blanket and the picnic basket, plus their best bathing suits, and headed to the bathhouse to change. Ray scoped out the beach and spread out their blanket not far from a lifeguard stand. He waited for the girls at the bottom of a wooden ramp onto the beach and then whistled his appreciation for their outfits. Bessie tossed her head back and strolled confidently past him. Hazel and Marion ran alongside an exuberant little Gracie, relishing her first steps in the sand. Maddie held on to the picnic basket as if it were a lifesaver and planted herself beside it, staring out to sea.

Gracie squealed with delight as she chased birds along the shoreline, running in and out of the waves with the surging tide. Even when she fell head-first into the crashing surf, she sprang back to her feet, laughing, filled with joy. Marion and Hazel took turns keeping an eye on her, amazed at how long it took to wear her out. She fell asleep after half a liverwurst sandwich, washed down with a lemonade Uncle Ray had bought her on the boardwalk. She slept with a smile of utter contentment that even managed to penetrate Maddie's dense personal fog.

"You gotta find yourself another man, Maddie. Someone stronger than the last one," Bessie said. She didn't have much tact. Maddie actually laughed in response.

"Yeah, how could any man resist all this," she replied, spreading her arms to display a pale, overweight woman who looked and felt much older than her 28 years.

"Maddie, there isn't a man on this whole beach who wouldn't turn his head for you if you just took a little better care of yourself and maybe showed them a little of the merchandise, if you catch my drift." Bessie's drift was easy to catch, but at least she made Maddie laugh.

Bessie pointed out a particularly handsome lifeguard in his tight white shorts and bright red sleeveless athletic shirt. Uncle Ray overheard her and struck a comical bodybuilding pose Maddie felt ought to have been captured on film. Then she remembered that stupid Brownie camera Lloyd always carried with him, and she drifted back into the dark lifelessness she had only briefly escaped.

As the sun set behind them, Ray and Marion Davidson walked the lively boardwalk of Seaside Heights hand in hand, with the Knowlton-Smyth clan. There were wheels of fortune and games of chance, sideshow barkers and penny arcades. Gracie was wide-eyed and beside herself, trying to take it all in. When the fireworks started to fill the sky, tears poured from her tiny eyes, as she was certain now that magic filled the air, just like her storybooks had told her.

When Gracie started school in September, Maddie felt a little relief. Between her job during the week and housework on weekends, she had less time to think about her sorry state of affairs. She spent most evenings helping her daughter with her homework. Her sisters were always ready to babysit whenever she had a date, so she accepted a few opportunities to be social. Her mother-in-law even introduced her to a salesman who reminded her a bit of her long lost Lloyd, but that date ended poorly, with him expecting Maddie to be a lot more grateful for his company than she was. It prompted an unexpected exchange when she came home disheveled and annoyed.

"What the hell happened?" the senior Mrs. Smyth wanted to know.

"Let's just say that George was not a gentleman," Maddie sighed, helping herself to a glass of her mother-in-law's illegal elixir.

"Pour me one and let's forget that sonofabitch," Grace responded with ironic tenderness.

That night Grace and Maddie had what might have been the longest and most heartfelt conversation either woman had ever had. They commiserated on the loss of their husbands and the loss of their youth. They laughed at the hardships brought about by a lack of education, and they drank to their determination not to let the same thing happen to the next generation of Smyth or Knowlton women. They decided to be candid with each other no matter what came their way and promised to protect each other from any damned fool who thought he knew better than they did. They plotted a way to make more money and said, "to hell with men." Grace told Maddie she would always be welcome to stay under her roof, and Maddie promised to take care of Grace in her old age. They would never mention that conversation again, but neither one of them would ever forget it.

Little Gracie did pretty well in school. She read everything she could get her hands on. She learned how to cook and sew at a very young age and made herself useful around the house. No one ever had to ask if her chores were done. She always did more than they asked her to do. She was a skinny little girl, but not sickly; mild mannered and well behaved, but nobody's doormat, either. She played hopscotch and jump rope with the neighborhood girls, but didn't let friends get too close. The Depression made families circle the wagons to make sure there was enough for their own. Her mother's depression caused an even greater isolation, but she counted herself lucky to have aunts nearby who were soon to have families of their own.

When Prohibition was lifted in 1933, little Gracie was only eight years old. Her mom got a part-time job as a waitress and barmaid at Casa Lido downtown and started spending most of her evenings there. Maddie's smoking and drinking aged her quickly, and her diet didn't help much. She and her mother-in-law had frequent arguments, and little Gracie looked forward to whatever time she got to spend with the Knowlton side of the family.

Aunt Carrie, Aunt Bessie, and Aunt Marion (who was actually her cousin but considered an aunt) all lived within walking distance of the Smyth household. Over the next few years, Gracie got used to visiting each of them as often as she could after school and offering to help with any chores they might need done so she could avoid going home. She was a good kid who never asked them any favors, so she was almost always welcome.

Carrie and Jake's family was growing, and Gracie just loved the little ones. Jake always had a pocketful of hard candy and saved her a couple of root beer barrels. Carrie really knew how to cook and gladly showed her niece a few secrets.

Bessie had married Breck, the iceman, who gambled and liked to curse. They never had kids of their own, so they talked to little Grace like an adult, telling her stories about the men in her mother's life. She tried not to blush and spent most of her time there dusting or sweeping since they didn't have anything else for her to do. She was relieved when Bessie took up knitting, because it gave them something wholesome to share, even though it didn't put an end to the stories.

Marion had married Len Whatley, another good man like Jake. They desperately wanted a child of their own but hadn't been able to have one. They offered themselves as foster parents and always had a couple of young ones in the house, sometimes with special needs. Gracie felt like she could really help there, mostly with cleaning and once in a while cooking. Marion actually had it all under control but liked having Gracie around and loved making her feel needed.

As Gracie entered her teens, things got even more stressful at home. Her grandmother noticed the way the male boarders had started looking at her and wanted no part of those possibilities. To make matters worse, her mother was spending more and more time away, and when she did come home, Maddie and her mother-in-law fought like cats and dogs.

"How dare you leave your teenage child in a house full of randy men?"

"You know damned well the only way I can pay what I owe you is to work every night and day!"

One Friday afternoon in early spring, Maddie showed up in Ray Davidson's car to pick Gracie up from school. Maddie seemed in a better mood than she had been in a long time, and Gracie was always happy to see Uncle Ray. Ray drove them out to Hightstown and dropped them off at Hazel Knowlton Morris's house for the weekend, with plans to pick them up on Sunday afternoon. Hazel's husband was traveling for business, and she was happy for the company. Maddie was five years older than Hazel, but the younger sister had her act together more. She lived in a clean, modest house with flowers in the yard and loved her neighborhood. She could walk to a green grocer down the street and sewed piecework at home for a small local uniform shop.

Maddie's health was failing her. She needed a place to get her thoughts in order and time to talk with her daughter. Hazel served them tea and cookies and then stayed out of their way.

"Listen Gracie, I'm sorry for the way I abandoned you. No, don't interrupt me. I have a lot to get off my chest, and you need to hear it before it's too late." Maddie finally told Gracie how her father had died and the impact it had on her the last ten years.

"Each of us has to come to terms with the reason we're here on this Earth, and I'm finally starting to understand that you were my best reason for being alive. Even if I haven't shown you much appreciation these last few years, I've been proud of you, every step of the way. I've got a sickness, honey. I'm not right … in my own mind." Mother and daughter cried. They hugged each other and held on tight. Hazel wept quietly to herself in the other room. The family had talked about sending her older sister to an institution, but people never came back out of those places the same. Maybe she was finally starting to wake up from her nightmare, and this was the turning point she needed. Hazel wasn't the only one who wanted to believe that.

They spent the weekend quietly at Hazel's cozy house, playing cards and talking about all the things Gracie could do with an education, while their hostess baked homemade chicken pot pies for dinner and squeezed fresh orange juice to serve with an egg pie she called a quiche for breakfast. They read magazines together and tried to make up for lost time. Grace reveled in her mother's attention, but she could not escape the fear that it was unlikely to last.

Six weeks later, Maddie suffered a massive heart attack and died before reaching forty years of age. Years of abusing alcohol and overeating, combined with heart disease and an unrelenting depression, had been too much for her.

Maddie's sisters felt it was extremely important to let Grace know she was not alone in this world, so they shared the one uplifting family secret no one had ever mentioned to anyone under eighteen years of age before. Whenever a Knowlton girl, or one of their close cousins, turned eighteen, they were eligible for what came to be known as The Yackers Club. If they failed to get enough votes, they would never know what they missed, but if they passed the vote, they were invited to join. It was a women-only organization whose sole purpose was to support each other and offer camaraderie through good times and bad. They met on a monthly basis to plan family picnics and holiday parties and to share in each other's triumphs or struggles. When one sister suffered an abusive husband, they were there to help her get rid of him. They shared hand-me-down clothing as the older kids outgrew it. They shared recipes, household tips, and each other's burdens. Given the special circumstances Grace now faced, they all agreed to make an exception to the minimum-age qualifying rule and voted her in at fifteen. At her first meeting, she listened shyly as her aunts openly discussed her future and reassured her she would always have a place with one of them. Most of these women had lived hard lives with little formal education. They were determined to see the next generation have it better than they did. They told stories about her mom and others who had passed before her and helped Grace feel a genuine connection to the Knowlton clan.

Grandmother Smyth had kept a roof over her head ever since she was born, but she made it clear she didn't want Grace living at the boarding house anymore. She may have been orphaned at fifteen years of age, but she wasn't abandoned. The Yackers Club decided she would spend the summer with Aunt Hazel in Hightstown while they worked out what was best for her in the fall. She trusted them and was grateful for their help. She could sew alongside her aunt for a few dollars that summer and save up a little pocket money. They both knew it was only temporary, but they were good company for each other, since Hazel's husband would be traveling quite a bit for the next few months. Hazel was a gentle soul who lived a quiet, peaceful life, comforted by fresh flowers and home-cooked meals. Her house was the perfect place for Grace to recover from her loss.

CHAPTER THREE

THANKS TO A SUMMER OF SEWING, Grace had three different skirts to make a good impression her first week in high school. Miss Foster, who taught home economics, specialized in sewing and noticed Grace's skill right away. When she found out Grace was an orphan, she took her under her wing, even letting her use one of the classroom sewing machines for an hour at the end of each day to make a little money on the side. Grace starting feeling pretty good about herself, when Miss Scozzaro, who worked in the office and always looked like she stepped off the cover of a fashion magazine, asked if she could make her something for a special occasion. Grace made her a two-piece navy blue suit with thin white satin trim in the style of Coco Chanel that looked like it was the work of the designer herself. She had gotten the fabric for three dollars and very stylish buttons for fifty cents. At Miss Foster's suggestion she asked for seven dollars, and Miss Scozzaro gave her ten. She had never held that much money before, and she liked it, a lot. This was still in the heart of the Great Depression, and very few people could afford new clothes, but word got around that there was a girl in Miss Foster's class who made really nice skirts for a couple of dollars, so the popular girls kept her busy and helped her build up some savings that fall. Eventually word got back to the principal, who chastised Miss Foster for running a cottage industry out of her classroom, but by that time Grace had saved up enough for a used Singer sewing machine of her own and starting working from the spare room at Aunt Bessie and Uncle Breck's house. They were only too happy to accept half her earnings in exchange for room and board.

Living with her aunt and uncle was actually kind of liberating for Grace. They didn't live by a very strict schedule and never imposed any rules. They both liked to go out to restaurants and bars every weekend, so she cleaned the house and had plenty of time to herself. Breck came home late almost every night and left for work before sunrise. She ate breakfast alone before going to school but had dinner with her Aunt Bessie almost every night. She got lessons on how to land a rich man, gossip about all the neighbors, and a never-ending fountain of family secrets. Bessie never once asked her about school, and Grace never bothered to tell her. She could stay as long as she didn't cause any problems, and she fully understood Bessie's frequent warning: "You'll be out on your ass the minute you do." She heard a little too often how her mother had been weak, just like her father, and that they had both failed miserably in life. "Nobody in this goddamned family ever amounted to anything anyway, so don't go thinking you're anything special." Aunt Bessie's words could be cruel, but Grace thought deep down she had a heart of gold, and she never lost sight of the kindness of letting her have the spare room in her house when no one else could take her in.

Trenton Central High School was a modern marvel and a world unto itself. There were classes and clubs, societies and sports, councils and associations, languages and arts, forums and special services. There were students of every ethnicity, race, creed, and socioeconomic background, reflecting the melting pot that was Trenton in its heyday. Grace had been a shy young girl, but she was quickly becoming a confident young woman.

"Hey, Shorty, you coming to the game tonight?" Alf Rossi was the co-captain of the varsity basketball team, and Grace liked the fact that he knew who she was, even if she wasn't crazy about her new nickname. She just smiled and shrugged her shoulders.

"Give me a kiss, Gracie, and I'll sink a basket for you," the tall, handsome young man pleaded.

"You can kiss my Irish ass, Alfie," Grace snapped back at him, blushing at her own attempt to imitate Aunt Bessie's salty language before the words had even left her lips.

"I would gladly take you up on that," Alf responded, puckering his lips.

"In your dreams, Alfie." She recovered her composure and hurried away, hoping he hadn't seen her blush.

As she turned the corner down the hallway by the auditorium, she heard a somewhat familiar song coming from one of the practice rooms. It was a slow and ironically sad version of FDR's theme song, "Happy Days are Here Again," and she was instantly drawn to it. When she looked in the window, she was surprised to see little Jimmy Norman at the piano. He was only a year younger, but small for his age. They were from the same neighborhood, and he had always been nice to her. She startled him when she opened the door.

"Don't stop, Jimmy. I didn't know you played piano." She smiled, taking a seat beside him on the bench. "C'mon, let's hear it again." She started singing the refrain in a clear and sweet soprano voice, which he accompanied, nervously at first, adding flourishes as both of them gained confidence. At the end of the song, she gave him a sisterly hug and had no idea the effect it had on him. He launched into an up-tempo arrangement of Nat King Cole's

"Straighten Up and Fly Right," and they both laughed their way through the chorus, "Cool down, Papa, don't you blow your top!" Grace gave Jimmy a peck on the cheek and almost danced out of the room. He was kind of cute, she thought. It was a shame he was just a little kid.

Little kids like Jimmy had been dropping out of school to join the armed forces ever since the Japanese bombed Pearl Harbor at the end of 1941. Trenton had sent a lot of her sons off to war. The high school held frequent events to support the troops, and everybody knew someone who had already lost a family member fighting overseas. President Roosevelt held fireside radio chats to keep the public informed, but for Grace, like most teenagers, it was almost impossible to keep up with current events. *First, the Martians landed at Grover's Mills, then we sank a German U-Boat off the coast of New Jersey. When did that zeppelin explode over Lakehurst? Where was America's First Defense Airport? Was there really an internment camp for Japanese, Germans, and Italians in Gloucester City, New Jersey? Who kidnapped Lindbergh's baby?* It was hard to tell truth from fiction with so many stories swirling all around. People only followed what affected them the most in their daily lives, on the job, in school, or with their families. That seemed like more than enough to bear at times, and Grace had already known her fair share of sorrow.

Luckily, she had mentors at school who encouraged her efforts. She concentrated on home economics because it made sense to her. Deep down, she didn't really think much of her Aunt Bessie's idea of marrying a rich guy, but she wasn't going to count on a poor guy, either. After losing her father and growing up with only stories about him, she wasn't quite sure what a good man was, but she knew she'd never settle for less. She could cook, clean, and sew well enough to care for herself, and she didn't need a man to prove it. *Still*, she thought, *it must be awfully nice to meet a guy who treats you right*.

Jacob Beers treated Grace's Aunt Carrie like a woman should be treated. Jake, as everybody called him, was a humble guy with a tender smile, pale blue eyes, a growing family, and a reputation for minding his own business. He stayed out of the family drama and provided for his wife and kids. He was loyal to his employers, showed up on time, and did more than they expected without complaining. When a job opened up to drive the newly appointed transportation commissioner, Jake applied and was hired on the spot. He had all the right qualifications. He was a conscientious driver who knew how to take good care of a vehicle. He was courteous, street smart, and, maybe most importantly, he could be trusted to keep whatever he overheard to himself.

One Friday in the fall of 1943, the commissioner gave Jake half the day off and two Saturday night tickets to the Latin Casino in Cherry Hill. He wanted to keep it a surprise from Carrie as long as he could. He wore a classic charcoal grey suit with a navy blue tie to work every day, and for Saturday night he could lose the chauffeur's cap, but he wanted to get Carrie a nice dress, and he knew who could help. He didn't like going over to Bessie's house. He wasn't much of a drinker and didn't curse, which seemed to be what his sister-in-law and her husband did best, but he hid his feelings and brought along a bottle of Canadian Club whiskey, knowing he'd be welcome. Bessie, Breck, and Jake were at the kitchen table when Grace got home from school. She was more than delighted to help, and Jake was thrilled to get out of there as quickly as he could. She was pretty sure she knew her Aunt Carrie's size and could make any last-minute adjustments on Saturday afternoon. She suggested they go to Dunham's when he told her he wanted this to be something special. They were only there for half an hour, though it felt a lot longer to Jake, when Grace spotted the perfect dress. She had turned down several others that he thought were nice, but she insisted he trust her. She knew what a dress should cost and wasn't going to throw away his money. She found an elegant evening dress in the perfect blue to match his tie. She was excited about how well it would go with a coat Aunt Carrie already had in her closet. He knew she had probably saved him quite a bit. He dropped her off with plans to pick her up around noon the next day, promising to pay for the fitting plus the babysitting.

"I can't thank you enough, Gracie. This has got to be special. Can you keep a secret? We're going to see Artie Shaw at the Latin Casino – a new nightclub in Cherry Hill!" Jake was clearly accentuating the positive, to quote a popular song, and Grace was thrilled to share his joy.

She loved babysitting Jake and Carrie's kids. The two older ones, Midge and Joey, didn't think they needed a babysitter, but they liked their cousin, and she did help them with their homework. The younger ones, Nicky and Avah, absolutely adored her. Aunt Carrie always left a wonderful home-cooked meal, and Jake always paid her more than she expected.

After her aunt and uncle left, dressed to the nines and smiling from ear to ear, Grace fed the kids and then settled down in the living room to listen to the radio with the younger ones. She would have paid them for the comforts she felt in their home and promised herself that someday, she'd have a home like theirs. The house was warm. You could feel the heat rise from the coal furnace through the grate in the living room floor. Grace pushed the spindle down on the floor standing ashtray, and the smell of Jake's pipe tobacco rose gently to her nose. Nicky was a cutup, making faces at Grace to see if he could get her to laugh. Avah, who was ten years younger than Grace, idolized her. They jitterbugged to the songs on the radio and took turns brushing each other's hair. It would have been hard to tell which one of them enjoyed it more.

"Do you have a boyfriend, Grace?" her curious cousin wanted to know.

"Well I do have my eye on one special guy," Grace teased her young admirer. She gave a wink and then launched them both into a frenzied rumba around the room until they collapsed on the sofa in a giggling breathless bundle.

There was no particular guy in her life, but she did date a couple of fellas. Of course, she had to keep it a secret from Aunt Bessie, who constantly warned her not to spread her legs for any Tom, Dick, or Harry. It hadn't been too bad in her sophomore and junior years. She was in the roller skating club and on the dance team and had a few opportunities to kiss and not tell as part of her extracurricular activities. But when she entered her senior year, they forbade her to join any clubs and insisted she work more and socialize less in order to pay her fair share of the growing household expenses. It didn't bother her too much, most of the time, but Sports Nite was coming soon, and that was a different story.

The social event of the year was more important that any single sport. The entire school was divided into red and black teams, competing, parading, singing and dancing, marching to beat the band. There was a mistress of ceremonies, and Marjorie Smith portrayed Miss America. Grace wasn't a jealous person, but if she could have traded places with anybody for a night, it would have been Marjorie Smith. Everybody loved her. She was beautiful and confident. She had the voice of an angel. She was a super student. And, on top of it all, she was just as nice as she was popular.

Grace slipped in and watched the program, enjoying it from the bleachers until the Roller Rhythm Revue came on. Watching them skate nearly broke her heart, remembering how much she had loved being part of them the previous two years. She was relieved when they skated away. She sneaked out of the auditorium as the band struck up a rousing patriotic march.

She passed two soldiers in uniform as soon as she was outside. One of them was leaning against the wall having a cigarette. The other one whistled his approval, looking her over slowly from head to toe as she walked by. She took it as a compliment. After all, this poor kid was probably going overseas soon to fight the Japs or the Germans, depending on where they sent him. The least she could do was give him a smile. Even though the war was all around her, Grace was a little less affected than her classmates. She had no father in her life; no brothers to lose in the war; no sisters pining for men who had left; no mother to work on a factory floor. Grace had been broke when times were good, so being broke now wasn't all that different.

By the time she graduated from Trenton Central High School, the effects of World War II were impossible to ignore. Only a little over fifteen percent of high school graduates went on to higher education in 1944. Now that Congress had passed the GI Bill, that number would continue to increase over the next few years with homeward bound, now college-bound, soldiers returning from overseas, but there wasn't much evidence of it yet. There weren't a lot of young able-bodied men living in Trenton, either. The factories that hadn't closed down during the Depression had converted to wartime production by now, and some employed more women than men.

Grace went to work fulltime, selling dresses at Dunham's Department Store in downtown Trenton. She doubled as a seamstress when they needed her for quick repairs to make a little extra pocket money. Her aunt and uncle started charging her rent as soon as she got her first paycheck, and she started saving whatever she could for her own apartment. In those days, good girls lived with their parents until they got married, but since Grace didn't have any parents, she didn't think that applied to her. All week long, all she did was work as many hours as she could get, and then come home to eat, sleep, and change her clothes. Her aunt and uncle tried to impose a curfew, but they were never home on the weekends to see what time she came in anyway. She didn't have many friends, but she did like to go out dancing with other girls from the store. Trenton had one of the first USO Clubs, and thousands of soldiers spent their weekend passes making passes at local girls like her. She was careful not to let it go too far.

One Saturday night, she was dancing with a sailor from St. Louis on his way to some place called Guam, when she spotted a familiar face in the crowd. Little Jimmy Norman was all grown up and looked pretty handsome in his army uniform with those incredibly shiny shoes.

"Hey, Jimmy. Nice to see you. Are you still playing the piano?" She flew out of St. Louis's arms back to the comfort of the neighborhood.

"Any time you want to sing," Jimmy replied shyly, almost swooning at the sight of her.

"Well then, I better start singing, before Uncle Sam takes you away." Grace grabbed his arm like an old pal and led him over to a couple of empty seats. They talked about the neighborhood. They talked about school. They talked about the fact that he had just enlisted in the army and was going to leave before graduating. She told him all about

Dunham's. He told her he was sorry when she lost her mom. She was touched by the fact that he cared. Before the night was over, they made plans to have dinner together. She didn't even realize he had asked her out for Valentine's Day until she wrote down the date in her diary that night. *Now that is one nice young man*, she thought. *It's a damned shame he's going off to war.*

Grace was surprised when she couldn't concentrate at work that week. She kept thinking about Jimmy. He remembered everything she had ever said to him. He paid attention to her like nobody ever had. He must have grown half a foot in the last year, and he really did look good in uniform. She started to blush, imagining him kissing her, and then tried to shake the idea out of her head. She caught herself humming the tune to "Straighten Up and Fly Right" as if it were their song. She couldn't wait to see him again.

He greeted her outside of Pete Lorenzo's Café on South Clinton Avenue with a dozen red roses. The hostess put them in a vase for her. Grace had never been to a steakhouse before and was intoxicated by the rich sizzling sounds. Jimmy's uncle was something of a mover and shaker in town, and this was the best place to eat as far as the politicians and bankers were concerned. They were seated at a dark romantic booth far from the kitchen noise, and after looking at the menu for a minute anxiously, Jimmy asked Grace if she would mind him ordering for both of them. She had no idea what to order anyway and liked the idea of him taking charge. He said just what his uncle had told him to say, confidently ordering salads and a porterhouse for two with two Doctor Swett's root beers, asking Grace if it was still one of her favorites. He had watched her enjoy one at a picnic they both attended in a neighbor's backyard years ago. She couldn't believe all he remembered and couldn't have been happier. Small talk turned to tender moments. They laughed together easily. The meal was sumptuous and savory. Both of them were fully satisfied and agreed they could skip dessert.

It was a little cool out when they left the restaurant, so she suggested he put his arm around her to keep her warm. Without ever deciding to, they strolled around town that way, on top of the world, up Market Street to the corner of Broad, where Jimmy said Al Capone got his shoes shined. They turned right onto Broad Street and headed toward the Old Barracks, where Washington had routed the Hessians. She kissed him in front of the statehouse before they hopped a Trenton Transit bus over to Olden Avenue and their Hobart Avenue neighborhood. They snuggled on the bus and looked like a young couple in love on Valentine's Day, even though this was their first actual date. It was still early when they got to her front door, and Grace knew her aunt and uncle wouldn't be home for hours. She decided it was worth the risk of getting caught and almost dragged Jimmy into her room, laughing as she kicked off her shoes and pulled off his coat, kissing him with complete abandon, as if she knew they would never have another chance.

Lots of young soldiers had begged their way into a young woman's bed by telling them how much they loved them and would miss them when they went off to war. Young women's hearts were littered around town by tales of the night before their handsome soldier or sailor shipped out. Grace and Jimmy's tender tryst was nothing of the kind. He truly had been in love with her for years, and she had absolutely no expectation of anything more than the warmth of their connection that night. He was gone long before the morning light, and she woke up feeling wonderful and hungry.

Aunt Bessie didn't suspect a thing until she noticed the roses.

"So? Who's Prince Charming?" she inquired.

"Oh, just a nice young man who works in the men's department," Grace lied quickly and with ease. "I think he's got a florist in the family; he gave bouquets to a bunch of us girls," she further covered the tracks.

"Sounds like he's a little light in the loafers, if you know what I mean," Aunt Bessie laughed, coughing from too many cigarettes the night before, as she spewed the latest euphemism for a homosexual. "Hey, we're better off with them tossing flowers at shop girls instead of messing with our boys at the front." Grace was just relieved that her lie had done the trick.

Meanwhile, Uncle Breck was delivering ice to Pete Lorenzo's Café. After he had hauled in the ten blocks Pete had ordered and chopped up the first two for the lunch crowd, Pete invited him into the bar for a drink and to pay him. That wasn't something Pete usually did, but Breck never looked a gift horse in the mouth. As he counted his cash and downed a shot of rye, Pete said casually, "Looks like your niece has found herself a nice guy."

"What are you talking about?" Breck replied, cracking his knuckles.

"She had dinner here last night with Eddie Norman's nephew. He's a nice kid. He just enlisted a few weeks ago and will probably ship out next month, but they looked pretty good together. She's a real looker, but then, I'm sure you've been chasing the boys away from her all year. She already graduated, didn't she?" Pete had never even spoken to Breck before, but any connection to Eddie Norman was worth cultivating. He was in the banking community and in tight with all the politicians. Breck barely managed to conceal his growing resentment. *This prick watches me break ice for him month after month and doesn't say a goddamned word, but the minute he thinks I might have a connection he can use, he's all, "Let's have lunch,"* Breck thought, but he kept it to himself. He knew who Eddie Norman was. He knew who everybody was and where the bodies were buried. The one thing he didn't know, was that his wife's niece was sneaking out of the house. He wasn't about to let her waste her talents on some dumbass soldier shipping overseas. He thanked Pete for the drink and got away from there as politely as he could manage.

He had to finish delivering ice to four more places, but he wasn't going home before he had a word or two with Eddie Norman's nephew. One of the veins in his neck started to pulse before he made it to the next stop. He hurled six blocks of ice like they weighed nothing and cut off the manager at Casa Lido before he had a chance to speak. He took the cash and kept on moving. Three more places to go.

Breck knew where the Normans lived, and as far as he could remember there was only one nephew old enough to be dating Grace. He rolled up his sleeves, and his face was nearly beet red when he banged on their door. Seeing Jimmy in uniform when he opened the door nearly lit a fuse. It was all Breck could do to resist grabbing him by the collar.

"I don't know who you think you are, but you sure as hell ain't good enough for Gracie," he spat threateningly.

"I'm in love with her," Jimmy blurted out.

"You're gonna stay the hell away from her is what you're gonna do." Breck got right in his face.

"I'm gonna marry her, is what I'm gonna do," Jimmy shouted right back at him.

"There is no goddamned way you are ever gonna see her again! I'll break every fucking bone in your body if you try!" Breck had grabbed him by now and was clearly enraged, but then he noticed the neighbors were watching. He threw Jimmy aside and stormed away, knowing he could get locked up if he hurt him in broad daylight.

"You've got no right to keep me away from her," Jimmy was screaming after him. "We're in love!" he screamed at the top of his lungs as Breck got in his truck and sped away.

When Breck told his drinking buddies what he intended to do to Eddie Norman's nephew, they all knew they had to talk him out of it. Eddie was a powerful guy who knew enough unsavory characters to protect his own. They reminded him that the kid had already enlisted and was bound to ship out soon. All he had to do was keep him away from Grace until then. That would be a lot easier than going up against whoever Eddie Norman had in his pocket. Breck eventually listened to reason and cooled down enough to come up with another plan. By the time he got home, Grace had already left for work, so he told Bessie everything he knew.

"I can't believe she lied to me. She's just like her mother," Bessie said. She was furious.

"The important thing is to keep them apart," Breck explained calmly. "If they get married, his family will pull her away from us while he's overseas. She's helping us pay the rent, and we don't want to lose that," he said, revealing his true motive. "Besides, she can do better than that. What the hell does she need with a soldier? She should go after a banker or somebody in big business. The kid's good-looking and built like a brick shithouse. We don't want her wasting her talents!" Bessie agreed wholeheartedly, so they plotted how to protect Grace from a guy who truly loved her.

Grace was surprised that her aunt and uncle were waiting for her when she got home from work. The conversation was about as awkward as it could get, with her not knowing how much they knew, and them not knowing how much she cared. They reminded her he was going off to war no matter how much she loved him. She apologized for not telling them about the date but admitted they hardly knew each other. Breck confessed he had gone a little overboard and threatened Jimmy to stay away, but he really thought it was for her own good. Grace was taken aback by her uncle's concern for her welfare, having never heard anything remotely like that from him in the two years she had lived with them. Part of her wanted to appreciate his gesture, but part of her didn't trust him. They were uncharacteristically familial and spoke about protecting her from bad decisions so she could live a full and happy life. She played the game and promised to be more truthful with them in the future, agreeing it was probably for the best not to see Jimmy anymore. She had never enjoyed a date more than that Valentine's Day with him, and she knew how he felt about her, but he *was* going off to war soon, and she had no idea if he would ever return. She had lost enough people she loved already and didn't want to fall in love with another, knowing she could lose him, too. She contented herself with the memory of having his arms around her, if only for one night.

Three weeks later, when the drama had subsided, Jimmy was waiting for her when she came out of work one night. She smiled at him as if nothing were wrong.

"Where have you been, stranger?" she asked as nonchalantly as she could.

"Grace. They wouldn't let me near you. I had guys following and threatening me. Your uncle said he'd break every bone in my body, but I just couldn't stay away." Jimmy was weak in the knees and had difficulty breathing. The truth was Breck had kept up a steady, careful campaign of intimidation, having him followed and harassed. As Breck explained it to Pete Lorenzo, who then explained to Uncle Eddie, Grace wasn't really in love with his nephew, but she didn't want to hurt him, and they all thought a little pretense allowed him to maintain his dignity. After all, he was shipping overseas soon, and they didn't want to break his spirit. Grace didn't know anything about it and definitely wouldn't have approved. She had real feelings for him in spite of her promise not to see him, but for his sake she tried to keep them to herself.

"It's okay, Jimmy. I'm not mad at you. That was my favorite Valentine's Day ever, and I'll never forget you." She had taken his arm and led him over to a stone bench in a downtown plaza near the department store. "When are you shipping out?"

"I'm leaving in two weeks, but we still have enough time to get married. I love you, Grace, and I want you to be my wife." He knelt before her with a ring box open in his hands. She was heartbroken, yet her eyes sparkled and she couldn't stop smiling.

"Ah, Jimmy." She punched him in the arm. "Why'd you go and do that?" She pulled him off his knee and made him sit beside her. "You know I love you, too." She said it like he was her brother. "But you're heading overseas, and some French girl is gonna steal your heart while I'm not looking. I'm not about to sit here waiting for some leftover soldier to return with French kisses all over him." She tried with all her might to lighten the mood and send him off without diminishing how much they meant to each other. He covered his face with his hands and willed himself not to break down in tears. She did her best to console him. "We had a wonderful time, but it was only one night. I'll tell you what. If you come back from the war and I haven't run off with a movie star by then, we can give it another try. What do you say?" Slowly but surely, he accepted that she wasn't going to marry him.

When he shipped off two weeks later, she spent the whole day crying.

It was another three months before she started to show, and by that time, Jimmy was long gone. There hadn't been any other men in her life, so she knew exactly when the seed had been planted. Breck said he knew a doctor who could take care of it, but she had no intention of aborting her child. She knew she was going to have to move out of Aunt Bessie and Uncle Breck's house even before they told her to pack her things, so she started looking for other lodging. She couldn't afford much on a salesgirl's salary, but luck intervened when the one cousin who was more like an aunt heard about her condition.

Aunt Marion and Uncle Len had a toddler named Lenny by then, and they were still foster parents for other children in need. They could use the help around the house and had a spare room for the mother-to-be. Grace couldn't believe how warm and welcoming they were. They were across the street from a church, so she went there pretty regularly, and it almost felt as if God himself had taken pity on her. There were a lot of young women in her condition in those days, whose husbands had planted a seed right before going off to war. So, while nobody said she was married, her family told anyone who asked that the father was overseas.

On November 5, 1945, the same day Colombia joined the United Nations, James Norman Smyth was born in Trenton, New Jersey. He was underweight, extremely fragile, and not long for this world. Grace lost her first child on February 5th, 1946, when he was barely three months of age.

CHAPTER FOUR

THE ONLY THING MISSING was a window. It forced her to look inside herself more deeply than she ever had. Uncle Len had recommended she spend time with the Bible. He had even marked passages he hoped would be of comfort in her time of sorrow. Neither he nor Aunt Marion wanted her to leave, but she needed a place of her own. She had no problem resisting Aunt Bessie and Uncle Breck's offer to take her back for a very reasonable monthly rent, now that she was without child.

She found a small apartment right on the bus route, off of Greenwood Avenue, close enough to walk downtown to work when the weather was nice. It was only a one-room place with an icebox and a hotplate, but she had her own bathroom. No matter how humble, it was hers alone. She wished she could have bought her own furniture, but beggars can't be choosers, so she gladly accepted a few modest pieces from her other aunts and uncles. Her sewing machine took up one corner of the room, with baskets from Aunt Myrtle to hold her spools and fabric. The kitchen table and two chairs Aunt Carrie and Uncle Jake had given her took up another corner, which she turned into a cozy nook with a checkered tablecloth and a creamy pink Lenox candy dish Aunt Hazel had given her. Of course, Jake filled it up with root beer barrels. Her prized possession was a bookshelf she had traded for dresses with a carpenter on Artisan Street in West Trenton. His wife and three daughters knew they had gotten the better end of the bargain, but between dime store novels and the public library, she kept that bookshelf filled. She felt it connected her to a much larger world.

One of her favorite books was *A Tree Grows in Brooklyn*. She thought it was no small coincidence that the author's last name was Smith, which was pretty close to Smyth, and the main character's last name was Nolan, which was pretty close to Knowlton. She read and reread one particular line in the story until it became her way of looking at life: "There are very few bad people. There are just a lot of people that are unlucky."

At twenty-one years of age, Grace had a job, an apartment of her own, a few nice dresses she had made herself, and a willingness to make the most of whatever life handed her. Whenever payday came around, that willingness was tested by the limits of her income and the cost of living on her own. On any given Saturday morning, she would put money into envelopes to pay her bills and mark everything down in a ledger like Miss Foster had taught her in home economics. Whatever she had left would determine the groceries she could afford to buy that week. The manager at Dunham's was glad to have her back. They paid her fifty cents an hour, which was ten cents more than minimum wage, mainly because she could sew in a pinch and knew how to sell the higher-priced dresses to a discerning clientele. Working thirty hours a week let her take home sixty dollars a month, and her sewing on the side netted her another twenty. After she took out for rent and bus money, plus a new pair of stockings, which were expensive during the war, she had ten to twelve dollars a week to live on. She bought a gallon of milk, a box of Lipton tea and Quaker Oatmeal for breakfast. A loaf of white bread was about ten cents, and eggs were fifty-nine cents a dozen.

Butter was expensive, so she only bought one stick and used it sparingly. Grandma Smyth had taught her you could do a lot with potatoes, and Aunt Carrie had shown her how to make a great potato salad with celery, onions, paprika, and mayonnaise. She made sandwiches of mayonnaise and potato chips because she couldn't afford meats or cheeses, and when she discovered tartar sauce in a jar for a few pennies more than mayonnaise, she felt like she was living well. Despite the fact that she never turned down an invitation to babysit, knowing it usually came with a home-cooked meal, she lost quite a bit of weight. She didn't date much that first year, either, but not for lack of opportunities. Her heart just wasn't strong enough to risk it too quickly, no matter what her aunts and the girls at work were telling her. As spring approached summer, the weather was especially nice, and she started feeling optimistic about her life again. Long walks by the river, watching birds in flight, and a date once in a while to watch the stars come out at night all helped Grace define her love of life.

On the first weekend of summer, she had a Friday night date and had planned to go down the shore with the same guy and his friends the next day – until fate intervened. They were in a corner booth at the Tremont House, listening to a popular local jazz combo, when she needed to use the restroom. Her smile went out ahead of her as she walked the length of the bar, not really watching where she stepped. Someone had casually put his foot in the aisle so she would have to step around him, and he gently put his hand on her elbow as she did.

"Careful, sweetheart. You almost fell for me," said the dark handsome stranger guiding her passage. She felt herself blush as she memorized his face, and she kept thinking about him while she waited for her turn in the ladies' room. She was sure he was watching her every move, but she didn't dare turn around to see him. When she started walking back along the bar, she was disappointed to see an empty seat where he had been. He caught her off-guard again, a little closer to the other end of the bar.

"Looking for someone, honey? What's your name?" he asked with a deep, melodic voice.

"I'm Grace," she stammered, finding it hard to look him in the eye.

"Nice to meet you, Grace. My name is Tony." He stuck out his hand as if to shake hers and handed her a matchbook with his phone number on it instead. "Call me when you get tired of dating little boys." With that he smiled warmly, looking her in the eyes before turning away. She watched him walk out of the bar without looking back.

She wasn't pretending when she said she felt flush and left her date at the bar. She said she was sorry but canceled her plans to join him for a day at the shore, too. She stayed home and read, with a smile on her face, trying to get her mind off of Tony. She ended up pacing the hallway near the telephone but decided she couldn't call him right away, for fear of seeming "easy." She didn't want to wait too long, either. Some other girl might steal him away.

The first time she called was on Sunday evening. When she asked for Tony, a woman with a thick accent responded by saying, "Tony no home," and abruptly hung up. She couldn't very well give up, since she hadn't even been able to leave a message, so she tried again on Monday evening when she got home from work. The same woman answered, but this time she added something. "Tony no home. Call back-a Tuesday." Grace got the feeling the woman had no idea what she was saying, but she couldn't wait to find out if her third call would be the charm. It was. Tony answered, and his voice was as warm and affectionate as if they had known each other for years. He was genuinely happy she called. He invited her to the movies on Friday night.

They met downtown at the Mayfair to see *The Razor's Edge*, starring Tyrone Power and Gene Tierney. It was no accident that Tony looked a lot like the star of the movie. He never mentioned it, of course, but even some members of the audience stared at him as they came in, whispering about the resemblance. He was a perfect gentleman, buying the tickets and popcorn, brushing off her seat with his handkerchief before inviting her to sit. They talked easily before the movie started and then stole glances at each other throughout the show. Afterward, he asked if she was hungry, and she took him by the arm for a downtown stroll. He took her to a small Italian place and ordered mussels marinara and a carafe of dry red wine. The waiter brought a basket of fresh crusty bread, and Grace made sure she ate delicately. Tony said something in Italian, and the waiter came back with a salad plate that had greens, tomatoes, meats, and cheeses. Tony served a full plate to his increasingly appreciative date. He asked her about her job and listened when she told him all about it. He asked about her family and she said something about having plenty of aunts, uncles, and cousins. He could tell when a question about her parents made her feel a little uncomfortable, so he changed the subject, asking about her favorite music, books, and hobbies. Other than that he had been in the army and now managed a grocery store on Market Street, she didn't know much about him.

She wondered if maybe it was the effect of the wine that made her want to kiss him, but he only gave her a peck on the cheek after walking her to her door.

"Are you free next Saturday, Grace?" he asked, holding one of her hands in both of his.

"What did you have in mind?" she answered, clumsily trying to flirt.

"Do you like to dance?" he asked with an amused expression, and she responded "yes" excitedly. "Great, there's a good band playing at the Hildebrecht next Saturday night, but I have to work until eight. Would you mind meeting me at the store?" She agreed, and he gave her a tender brief kiss on the lips.

It was hard for her to concentrate at work on Monday. Tuesday was even worse. She was dying to tell somebody all about him but also enjoyed keeping it a secret. She decided to visit Marion after work on Wednesday, knowing she had a standing invitation for dinner. Len left them alone when they finished eating so they could enjoy a little girl talk.

"He's Italian and he looks just like Tyrone Power. He was in the army, but now he manages the American Store on Market Street."

"I think I've seen him," Marion pondered. "Yes, I have. He's very handsome, so you better be careful."

The conversation went on for an hour like that, with Grace assuring Marion that he was a true gentleman, and Marion warning her they all act like that until they get what they want. Marion laughed out loud when Grace told her she sounded like Aunt Bessie. They were both more optimistic than that, even if he was Italian. They were known to have a way with the ladies.

Tony had a way with the ladies, alright. Grace got to the market at eight on the dot and watched him interact with an elderly patron.

"Did you find everything you were looking for, Mrs. Allen? Let's see, that's a pound of bologna, two tomatoes, one loaf of bread, a nice head of lettuce, and a jar of Hellman's. Looks like somebody is having a picnic." He winked at her. "How about a nice cake for dessert? You want it to be special, right?" He counted the numbers on his fingers, adding them in his head, then rang up the total on the register.

As Grace watched the old woman blow Tony a kiss on her way out the door, she realized she hadn't taken the cake with her. She was ready to mention it when Tony put his finger to his lips. He closed the door behind his patron, then ushered his date to a seat behind the counter, while he took off his apron and tidied up a bit.

"I know, Gracie. You're wondering about the cake. It's a little game I play. I sold that cake four times today and nobody bothered to pick it up. I usually only sell it twice before I take it home for my mom and my sisters, but you can have this one." He tied a ribbon around the cake box expertly.

So, he lived with his mom and his sisters. He was so charming that Grace would have bought the cake too, if she didn't have to watch every penny. She was going to take him up on that cake and made a mental note to come back for it.

"That's a beautiful dress, Grace. Somebody should take you out dancing." He offered his arm as they left the store and hailed a cab out front with a sharp piercing whistle. She was going to suggest they walk, to save money, but she liked that he was willing to spend a little on their date. She had never been to the Hotel Hildebrecht before, but it had an upscale reputation, and she was looking forward to seeing it. The doorman opened the taxi door, and Tony smiled at her taking in the ambiance from the moment they walked through the entrance. He slipped the *maître d'* a five-dollar bill to lead them to a well-placed table for two near the center of the ballroom. She felt like everyone's eyes were on them, and he knew what she was feeling.

"What good is dating a gorgeous gal if nobody sees you do it?" As soon as the band started playing, Tony stood and asked Grace for a dance. They moved well together, gently swaying to a ballad. They had no sooner found their footing than the whole joint started jumping. After a few fast-paced numbers, to which they jitterbugged and jived, they made their way back to the table, and Tony signaled a waiter.

"Gracie, how about a high ball?" She had never had one before and thought it sounded swell. Tony ordered two and offered her a cigarette, lighting one for each of them. She didn't smoke, as a habit, but enjoyed this special occasion. Several well-dressed couples smiled and nodded at them in passing, making her feel she belonged. One tall handsome guy in a tuxedo stopped to shake Tony's hand.

"Give my best to your brother, Don. My money was always on him for a knockout." Tony explained his older brother had been something of a local sports celebrity – a "golden glove" boxer, whatever that was. He had been in the army, too, but now he worked for General Motors and lived across the river in Pennsylvania.

"You'll like him and his wife, Jo," Tony said, as if it were already understood she'd be meeting his family. It made her feel Marion's warnings weren't really all that necessary. The evening could not have been more fun, nor he more of a gentleman. He tipped the doorman to hail them a cab and had the driver idle at the store while he picked up Grace's cake. She considered inviting him in when they got to her place but was a little too nervous. He interrupted her train of thought to offer the cake in exchange for another date. She happily accepted and gave him a long, strong goodnight kiss.

On Sunday morning, as she sat eating cake for breakfast with a cup of tea, she smiled, remembering how they had danced the night before. All the boys she had ever dated, with the exception of Jimmy Norman, had tried to get her to fool around as quickly as they could. Tony treated her so differently that it made her want him more. Maybe that's what he was doing. *Is he seducing me?* She wondered. She had read enough tawdry tales to look for telltale signs. He was dark and handsome. Not very tall, but tall enough. He had a regular job, so there was no mystery there. He lived with his mom and his sisters, so he couldn't be a gigolo, could he? She couldn't afford to pay him, if he was. She laughed at the thought, amusing herself and enjoying the heck out of her delicious ill-gotten cake.

Tony stopped by Dunham's on Tuesday afternoon to apologize in advance for having to break their Friday night date. The store owner needed a full inventory for the insurance company and some potential investors. Grace couldn't hide her disappointment, or her surprise, when he suggested she come over to his house on Saturday afternoon to meet his mom and pop. She was nervous the rest of the week.

"Hi, you must be Grace. I'm Tony's sister Jeanne. He told us to expect you. He's still stuck at the store but should be home soon. Come in, please." Jeanne led her to the kitchen, where the lady of the house, who was stirring several pots and pans, motioned to a seat at the table, and Grace sat down, folding her hands in front of her. When Jeanne said it was nice to meet her but she had to run, Grace's knee started bouncing up and down uncontrollably, and she anxiously bit her lower lip.

"You hungry?" the short gray-haired old woman asked – then answered herself, without waiting.

"I'm-a make you a san-a-gwich." Concetta Calu, Tony's mom, proceeded to slice what they called a bat bread lengthwise at the table while smiling at Grace. She drizzled a couple tablespoons of rich olive oil and red wine vinegar on the bread and spread it out with a knife. She crumbled prosciutto and salami, then added sharp cheese, onions, peppers, lettuce, and tomatoes, before topping it off with crushed oregano and putting the whole thing on a plate in front of her guest.

"*Mangia,*" she said, miming putting food in her mouth.

"It's so big. Do you mind if I cut it in half and take the rest with me?" Grace explained with motions, figuring there was enough for a whole week's lunches. Just as she was cutting the san-a-gwich, a stout-looking gentleman in work clothes came in the back door.

"Frank – this-a Tony's girl, Grace." Concetta was close to the limits of her English, making an introduction. When Frank asked what she was doing with the knife, Concetta explained she was taking half for later.

"I'm-a call you Scotch," Frank said with a laugh, shaking Grace's hand. The Irish bricklayers he worked with always told him Scottish people were very frugal. He liked her right away.

"Poor girl, she's a *morta fam,*" he whispered to his wife, saying she was dying of hunger. They both watched her eat with pleasure, smiling at the first girl Tony had ever invited to their home. Even though she could hardly have a conversation with them, the room started feeling warmer with each bite she took. Her knees stopped bouncing up and down, and the smells coming from the pots and pans on the stove were so wonderful she felt like crying for joy. Frank disappeared and came back with a jug of his homemade wine. He poured a little for each of them. They sat down together at the table, clinked glasses, and toasted their good fortune, just as Tony walked in. He gave his mom a kiss, first, and handed her a cake in a box. Then he kissed his pop on the cheek before moving over to sit next to Grace. He greeted her with a kiss, too, as if it were the most natural thing in the world to do. She had never felt more at home in her life. Speaking between Italian and English with Tony doing the translations, they sat there until the sun went down, getting to know each other. Concetta made Grace taste everything she was cooking and couldn't believe she had never tasted half the dishes they ate on a regular basis. What did she eat, anyway? Nothing much, Frank commented, calling her "skin and bones" in Italian, which Tony translated as "needing more meat." By the time Jeanne came back with her other sisters, Fran and Mary, their mom had turned the kitchen table into a banquet table for their most welcome guest. Tony cut his sisters off abruptly when they started speaking in Italian.

"Hey, it's tough enough on Grace to understand mom and pop without having to wonder what the hell you three are saying about her!"

Grace had never felt so protected before and couldn't believe how wonderfully they treated her. When she and Tony finally made a move to leave, Concetta hugged and kissed her goodbye, and Frank caught her at the door, handing her a paper bag.

"Hey Scotch, no forgetta you san-a-gwich."

She kissed Frank on the cheek. She was welcomed into the family before Tony had even proposed. Concetta was not going to let this girl get away. She and Frank both made up their minds that night, and they told Tony so the next day at Sunday dinner. It didn't take him long to come around.

Grace knew things were getting serious, and there was one thought she couldn't bear. What if he didn't want her once he knew about her past? With as many cousins, aunts, and uncles as she had, he would eventually find out, so it wasn't fair not to tell him now, and that's what she knew she had to do, as soon as possible, no matter what it cost her. She invited him to dinner at her place and decided to cook for him the very first time. She wasn't sure what she was more nervous about – cooking dinner after tasting his mother's cooking or telling him about an unmarried pregnancy and a lost child.

She served him Aunt Carrie's potato salad with a thick slice of baked ham she had heated on the hot plate and an ice cold beer she knew he liked. The meal went over well, so she launched into a heartfelt expression of her feelings for him and his family. She didn't have to wait long for his reaction. He was a better man than that.

"Grace, honey. I'm so sorry you have been through so much pain in your life. I'm here to share your pains from now on. You can count on me. I love you, sweetheart." He held her, sobbing, in his arms. They were inseparable from that night on. He proposed to her a week later on bended knee with a ring box in his hands.

In September, about a month before their wedding, Trenton celebrated what was called "The Feast of Lights." It was held in an Italian neighborhood called Chambersburg. Concetta and the girls looked forward to socializing with other friends and family. Grace thought it would be a good opportunity for them to meet some of her family, too, so she invited Marion and Len to join them. They had already met Tony and were helping the couple plan their wedding, but this would be the first time they had met the rest of his family.

Frank didn't like Chambersburg. It was full of too damned many Italians, and he wouldn't let his family live there. He came to America for the melting pot. If he had wanted to spend his life around a bunch of Italians, he would have stayed in Italy. He indulged Concetta's and his daughters' need to connect with their friends and family a few times a year, but warned them not to make a habit of it. Before his son Tony had met Grace, Frank had a serious falling out with his own brother, Tony, for whom his son was named. For years, Frank had given his brother money out of every paycheck to help the folks back home. He did that in spite of how tough the Depression was on a stonemason and how many kids of his own he had to feed. In time, when relatives from the old country visited, they praised his kid brother Tony and spat on the ground when they saw Frank. Tony had never told them that Frank pitched in. Nobody knew for sure if Tony had ever put in a dime of his own while he was sending them Frank's hard-earned money. Frank reminded his kids to avoid that side of the family as often has he could.

Tony's sister Mary explained to Grace and Marion that this festival was the Festa della Madonna in honor of Our Lady of Casandrino. "The blessed mother Mary," Len interjected as he eavesdropped on her explanation. Mary was impressed with Len as they continued a conversation about the Bible. Concetta took Grace and Marion by the arms and introduced them to zeppoles at a local vendor's stand. Marion loved the lightly fried Italian puff pastry filled with butter and honey. Concetta was happy to share her recipe. Fran and Jeanne grabbed Grace by the hand and told her to watch what their older brother Donny was doing. Grace had met him earlier that night, and he and his wife seemed just as nice as Tony had told her they would be. Donny had a five-dollar bill in his hand, and he was approaching the statue of the Madonna as a group of men carried her down the street. They paused to let him pin the bill to the decorative blanket at the feet of the Virgin. He announced to the crowd it was for the good fortune of his brother Tony and his fiancé, Grace! Everyone cheered, and she blushed with pride as Tony stood beside her and put his arm around her waist, pulling her in for a kiss. There was music and fireworks, dancing and food for people of all ages, right there on the streets of the city. Grace felt like she was a child again and the festival was for her more than anyone. Concetta introduced her to every cousin, aunt, and uncle she could find, beaming with pride at her son's bride-to-be.

When Tony went to introduce his older brother to Len, Len already knew who he was.

"Donny Calu, Golden Gloves? I knew I remembered that name from somewhere. I saw you fight at the armory. You had one heck of a right cross." Len had a passion for sports that was equal to his love of the Bible. Grace and Tony both marveled at how well their families got along.

They had one small hurdle to overcome before the parish priest would allow them to get married at Sacred Heart Church, and Frank was embarrassed to have caused it. Early last spring they had announced from the pulpit that there was a serious problem with starlings. Frank loaded a shotgun and went up on the roof of the church to blast the birds away. It worked like a charm, and the priest even sang his praises the following Sunday at mass. Unfortunately, the next time it rained, there were a thousand tiny holes in the roof and raindrops drenched the entire congregation. Tony paid a small crew to patch all the holes and prayed the birds would stay away, at least through October 4th.

Marion's son Lenny was the ring bearer and Aunt Myrtle's daughter Diane was the flower girl. Tony's sister Jeanne was Grace's maid of honor, and Ray Davidson gave away the bride. Grace was a vision in her white silk gown, and there were no dry eyes in the church. The bride and groom honeymooned in Montreal, Canada, because Tony wanted to show his bride as much of the world as he could give her.

CHAPTER FIVE

THEY SPENT THEIR FIRST NIGHT as husband and wife in New York City at the Biltmore Hotel near Grand Central Station so they could board the train to Montreal the next morning. They didn't get to see much of New York that night, but Tony promised to bring Grace back to the Biltmore when he saw how excited she became hearing that the gardens were converted to an ice skating rink in the winter. He had never been on skates before and secretly hoped to postpone that trip forever.

Upstate New York and Vermont looked beautiful through the windows of a slow-moving train, and the sleeper car was a cozy place to get acquainted with a modicum of privacy. They pulled into the Bonaventure train station mid-morning and walked across the boulevard to the Hotel Le Saint James, where they would spend the whole week in luxury.

The first twinge of pain came as Tony bit into an incredible Chateaubriand they shared their first night in old Montreal. It had been a mild discomfort leading up to the wedding, but he didn't think much of it and ignored the warning signs. He continued to ignore it the next day as they visited the Cathedral of Notre Dame and the Place-d'Armes. They dined elegantly that night on Prince Edward Island mussels in a white wine broth, then took a carriage ride around Victoria Square, and the bride felt she finally had her fairy tale adventure.

When she rolled over in bed the next morning to look at her real-life Prince Charming, the entire left side of his face was swollen from an abscessed tooth. They didn't know enough French between them to ask for what they needed, but the concierge could clearly see the problem as they stood in front of him, so he made the necessary arrangements. In the taxi on the way to the dentist, Tony still tried to tell her it was no big deal. She put her head on his shoulder and instinctively squeezed and rubbed his hand in hers forcefully, taking his mind off of the pain. The dentist removed the source of his throbbing ache, and the swelling subsided fairly quickly. He couldn't eat anything solid for the next couple of days, but she liked waiting on him, and they both enjoyed a little rest once the excitement of the wedding began to fade.

They started making plans for the future. They both wanted a family. Tony wanted to move out to the suburbs. He was going to have to find another job, since the American General Store was about to become ACME, and he didn't have much faith in the idea of a supermarket. He was thinking about selling insurance, since those guys made a pretty good penny. Grace said she could keep working at Dunham's until she had their first baby and then, after that, she could sew at home for piecework like she had with Aunt Hazel. All she had to do was find a garment manufacturer who needed a seamstress. He wanted a nice backyard with enough room to plant a garden and a basement where he could build a workbench. She wanted a nice kitchen and a dining room, plus a spare room where she could sew. First they had to buy a car and move out of her apartment. He had enough savings to buy a car, and they could use the GI Bill to get a home mortgage. She had heard about a new development called Mercerville that might be perfect.

By the time Thomas J. Calu was born in August of 1948, they had the dream house, a new car, and a thoroughly wonderful life together. Most important of all, Tommy was a happy, healthy child they each welcomed in their own special ways. Tony was going to make sure his son grew up smart. Nobody was going to take advantage of him. Grace was going to make sure her son knew he was loved. He was never going to doubt it for a minute.

The house on 240 Lowell Avenue in Mercerville cost them thirteen thousand, six hundred dollars. It was a small fortune at the time, but the GI Bill secured them a mortgage and taxes were pretty low, so their monthly payment was around a hundred twenty dollars. That seemed like a lot to Grace, but Tony reassured her he could handle it. It was a two-bedroom, one-bathroom Cape Cod with a living room, dining room, kitchen, and basement. It had a long front porch and good-sized backyard. There were only a few other houses on their street so far. The rest of the neighborhood was still covered in woods.

Grace had stopped working when Tommy was born, so she had a chance to meet the new neighbors as they moved in. Carl and Lillian Karlberg moved in right next door. They had a pretty daughter, Carla, who was two years older than Tommy. Grace welcomed them to the neighborhood with a casserole and couldn't wait to introduce them to Tony. Lillian very formally reciprocated for the casserole by inviting them over for cocktails on Friday at eight o'clock, sharp. It promised to be a social event unlike those they normally attended.

Tony had dropped off Tommy at his mom and pop's place on Jackson Street earlier in the day while visiting a couple clients in the old neighborhood. He was doing pretty well selling life insurance policies to all of his old American

Store patrons, but Grace made him promise not to try and sell anything to their new neighbors.

"All right, honey. At least not until I get to know them," he teased her as she tried on a second and third dress before deciding what to wear for "cocktails."

They rang the doorbell at eight sharp and Carl answered, wearing a cardigan and smoking a pipe. Once they were seated in the tastefully furnished living room, Lillian emerged from the kitchen, dressed in a bright flowery silk blouse over expensive-looking black slacks. She had a black silk bow in her fiery red hair, and she was carrying a tray of appetizers hot out of the oven.

"This is your husband? I thought you had an Italian gardener when I saw him planting those hedges last week." Lillian extended her hand to Tony as if her comment was completely innocent and natural. Carl quickly offered drinks, and Tony couldn't wait to see how fast those hedges would grow.

The conversation was pleasant enough, but it was quickly apparent that they were from different places and heading different places in life. Carl was an architect, working with a firm in Princeton. He was soft spoken, very intelligent, and genuinely friendly. He put both his guests at ease. Lillian was a bit more high-strung. She prided herself on keeping up a very active social life, mainly in Princeton, and according to her, this was only going to be a temporary home until they could find something more suitable. She did enjoy the backyard and explained that she would have her one cigarette a day there every afternoon at four p.m., weather permitting. At ten o'clock sharp, as if it were already understood, Lillian stood to dismiss her company with a "thank you for coming" and an attitude of "let's not try to do this again any time soon." Carl appeared sad to see them go, but Tony and Grace were both relieved to be going home. Their relationship would remain friendly but formal from that evening on.

Good fences make for good neighbors, Tony laughed to himself the next day, watering the privet hedge he had planted along the full length of both sides of his backyard a few weeks earlier. His next two projects were to build a small fireplace and barbecue grill in the yard and then put up a chain link fence across the back line of his property. His father was going to help him with both.

Grace couldn't say what it was about her father-in-law that she liked so much. He hardly spoke any English, so they didn't talk very much. He showed up one afternoon with a pair of dead rabbits that he expected her to cook. He had walked from downtown Trenton out to Mercerville while hunting along the seven-or-so-mile hike. He wouldn't go in the house since Tony wasn't home and only grudgingly accepted a glass of lemonade Grace brought out to the front porch for him. When Tony showed up, he led him to the backyard and they started arguing about the best spot to put the fireplace and how to build it. When Tony went to pick him up the following Sunday morning, Frank was waiting with his wife and a picnic basket full of food, plus a bag of cement and a pile of red bricks.

While Frank and Tony spent the afternoon building the chimney and covering it in cement, Concetta gave Grace cooking lessons. While the boys argued and laughed at each other, both trying every shortcut they could find, and having to patch up their mistakes, the girls smiled tenderly at each other, slowly coaxing the best out of the freshest ingredients and blending them into a delicate and delicious sauce with homemade meatballs and pasta *al dente*.

After the boys washed up with the hose out back, they came in just in time for dinner to be served. Tony couldn't believe how good his house smelled. Frank couldn't believe he didn't have any wine to go with his meal.

"You'll just have to make do with a beer, Pop," Tony teased, handing him a can of Schmidt's, to which Frank responded by joking to his wife in Italian. "We didn't even raise him good enough to give it to me in a glass." Grace didn't understand the words, but she could read Frank's meaning, so she handed him a nice tall glass and he smiled appreciatively.

Over dinner, Frank shared stories of the old world, which Tony translated in between grateful mouthfuls of his mama's cooking, as she passed the secrets on to his wife. One secret Grace wondered about was the origin of her husband's full name, Anthony Tone Calu. Didn't they realize that was like calling him Tony twice? Gradually it came out. When the nurse asked Frank and Concetta about a middle name for their son, they misunderstood and thought she wanted to know what they would call him, so they both said "Tone," and that became his middle name. They all laughed good-naturedly at it that night, and Tony made her promise not to tell their new neighbors. It was tough enough being an Italian gardener without being known as "Tony, Tony."

The neighborhood kept growing as Tommy became a toddler. There were the Parkers and the Clarks by then, both big families on the other side of the street. There were the Rockells and the Wrightleys, the Bullocks and the Schipskes, and half a dozen other families with two or three kids belonging to each.

Even though Tony hadn't thought people would ever go to a supermarket, it was a huge success, and he shopped there like everybody else did. Of course, he still went to a favorite butcher, baker, and green grocer, but for canned and dry goods, you couldn't beat the prices offered by the bigger stores.

There weren't any restaurants in the suburbs yet, so whenever they could afford a night out, Tony and Grace would drop Tommy off at his grandparents and eat somewhere downtown before catching a movie or a live combo. It would be a while before they had any other social life beyond his family and their occasional night out. Grace saw less and less of her family and missed them quite a bit. Marion and Len did visit them in Mercerville a couple times, and Jake and Carrie brought the kids over once, but it was hard getting together when you weren't in the same neighborhood anymore and everybody's lives kept getting busier all the time.

Frank died suddenly in April of 1952, and Tony took charge of helping his mom. With all of his brothers and sisters out on their own by then, he knew she would need a new place to live. Grace suggested she move in with them, but Tony knew his mom wouldn't be happy there. She clearly loved Grace and her grandson, but she needed the shops, sights, and smells of a city to keep her going or else she'd just waste away without her husband beside her. They found her a nice small apartment on Hobart Avenue, not far from where Grace grew up, so it had the added advantage of getting her closer to her family whenever she visited his. Sunday dinners became a tradition, so Concetta would never get too lonely.

It was at one of those Sunday dinners that Tony's older brother Donny told him about Fairless Steel. Donny lived in Pennsylvania and drove across the river to work in Trenton at the General Motors Auto Parts Plant, but he heard about a big new steel mill opening on the Pennsylvania side of the river and suggested Tony look for a job there.

Tony had wanted to go to college when he came back from the war, but his family needed him to pitch in, and so he had gone to work. He had started thinking about it again recently since he could sell insurance at night while taking a few classes, but now it seemed too late for anything like that. The U.S. economy was growing fast, but guys who had been through the Depression weren't about to gamble with their family's groceries when there were decent paying options to be had.

It wasn't a very far commute, and luckily he had a reliable car. He had bought his grayish-green four-door Kaiser Special back in 1947 for eighteen hundred sixty-eight dollars. It ran well as long as he kept the oil changed, so he was religious about it. The Fairless Plant of U.S. Steel was about fifteen miles from his doorstep. They hired him on the spot as a security guard and radio dispatch operator, since he had experience in the army and didn't mind shift work.

When Grace found out she was pregnant again, he was happy to have a Blue Cross and Blue Shield Medical plan as well as a damned good salary. There were a lot of men in Mercerville who worked factory jobs. They all promised a great pension for retirement and every single man looked forward to it.

Late one afternoon that spring, Tony was trying to get a garden started when his younger brother Johnny showed up to surprise him. There could not have been a more welcome guest. This pregnancy had been a little hard on Grace, and it brought back some of her old fears about the baby's health. Tommy was a fully rambunctious youngster by then, and she was only too happy to let his father and uncle entertain him.

"You haven't even offered me a beer yet? What's the matter with you, Tone? Grab one for the kid while you're at it." Grace heard Johnny tease his older brother as she started to walk back into the house.

"Hey, Tone," Grace said, trying out his middle name for the first time, "why don't you throw a couple steaks on the grill while I make a salad?"

Tone gave her an appreciative wink in passing and then handed his brother a beer. They took turns bouncing Tommy on their knees and giving him a couple sips. Within half an hour, the four-year-old was down for the count, so they laid him on a blanket in the grass beside them and continued the conversation while the grill got hot.

"I'm heading up to Providence, Rhode Island. I've got a buddy stationed there who says there's all kinds of opportunity for a savvy sailor like myself." Johnny had just gotten out of the navy, and Tone couldn't stand the idea of him moving so far away already.

"You just got here, for Christ's sake. Pop's gone, and Mom could use a little help. Why don't you stick around awhile? There are plenty of jobs here, and besides, I finally have the time to teach you how to fish."

"You teach me? You sonofabitch. I can outcast you any day of the week!" Grace loved hearing Tony laugh so hard. She hoped Johnny would stick around, too. But he didn't. Even still, he did have a lasting impact on them in two very specific ways. From his visit on, she started calling her husband "Tone" or "Tony" interchangeably depending on her mood, and when their second child was born in June, even though she had momentarily considered naming him Norman, she decided his name would be John, like his uncle.

Little Johnny was born into a rapidly growing neighborhood. Mrs. Parker also had a son they named John a few days before Grace and Tony's second son was born. The Rockells' second child, Randy, was born a month later.

There were more and more families with children on Lowell, Eaton, Elmore, Fenwood, and Grayson Avenues now. There were Irish and Italians, English and Germans, Jews and Gentiles, Catholics and Protestants. These kids would grow up and play together in the remaining wooded areas, plus the ballfields and school playgrounds, as downtown Trenton started to empty into suburbs like this one in Mercerville.

New factories opened up, like Congoleum, making tile and linoleum flooring. The David Sarnoff Research Center for RCA was in full swing just five miles away on the road toward Princeton. There was a palpable excitement for young couples like Grace and Tony who had lived through the Depression and could now see their dreams coming true. They had even bigger dreams for their children.

CHAPTER SIX

SOME DREAMS ARE MORE PRACTICAL than others. In 1953, when Tommy entered kindergarten, the teachers focused on building a foundation for real-world skills. They let children play, but they taught them to associate play with the colors, shapes, and sizes in their everyday lives. Blue was like the U.S. Postal mailbox. Red was both a barn and a stop sign. Yellow was the Jersey corn they had eaten all summer long. Green was the color of their lawns. They guaranteed reading readiness alongside building blocks and outdoor experiences. They concentrated on personal hygiene and even introduced financial responsibility by teaching students how to count their coins.

By the time Johnny entered kindergarten five years later, something had changed dramatically. Even though teachers still concentrated their efforts on the same basic principles, the students expected to be entertained. Television was now as common in the average suburban home as radio had been for the previous generation, and "Disneyland," which first appeared in 1954, had by now captured the imagination of Tommy's kid brother along with most of his classmates.

When you wish upon a star,
Makes no difference who you are.
Anything your heart desires will come to you.

Grace was thrilled when little Johnny announced, at the tender age of five years old, that he intended to become a writer. Tony wondered out loud how he'd ever make a living and decided to balance Disney's optimism with the teachings of the Holy Roman Catholic Church by taking both boys to Sunday mass and enrolling them in catechism.

Grace had tried to join the church, but she had a little problem with the pastor's assertion that the only way she could speak with God was through him, in the act of confession.

"No offense, Father, but I can speak directly to God whenever I want to. He comforts me when I pray and shows me his beauty in the nature that surrounds us."

Father Greco and the church he represented at the time would not tolerate that kind of thinking. "You will never belong to the Holy Roman Catholic Church unless you accept the authority of the priest and confess your sins to God Almighty, through me!"

Tone walked both boys to church every Sunday and sat silently listening to a mass in Latin, finding solace in a childhood ritual he had never questioned. He respected his wife's decision, even if he didn't quite understand it. Priests were like policemen to him. It was easier to do what they said, even if you suspected, as he did, that they didn't know their ass from a hole in the ground.

Sunday breakfast was always waiting for them when they got home. Eggs over easy, hash brown potatoes, bacon, and buttered toast. Grace would ask about the sermon, which none of them remembered. Johnny would paraphrase the parables while Tone and Tommy ate. Then Tommy would run out the door to meet Jimmy Clark and head into the woods, a few blocks away.

"Tommy, don't get any stains on your good pants, and be back here by two o'clock. We're going to Grandma's for Sunday dinner."

Johnny designated himself Grandma's little helper in the kitchen and promised he would take her to California when he grew up. She could finally visit her cousins and see the vineyards they raised. He told her they would need three horses: one for him and two for her, because she was too big around the middle for one. He would try to get his arms around her waist every time he told her, and she would hug him laughing as if she were hearing it for the first time, every time he said it. Grace tried to help Concetta, but she could tell that her mother-in-law lived to cook Sunday dinners, so she contented herself with the wonderful food and tried to pick up whatever cooking tips she could without getting in the way.

First came an antipasto with cured meats and cheeses, some olives, artichokes, and roasted red peppers. Homemade ravioli came next, stuffed with ricotta and topped with a rich red gravy that had been cooking all morning. Meatballs and sausage were served alongside it, with crusty bread to sop up the juices; then a salad course, including fennel, cleansed the palate; and a clear broth with fresh grated parmesan and crushed black pepper got them ready for a delicate chicken or fish dish. Finally, a fruit plate helped them digest their good fortunes, accompanied by coffee and a touch of anisette.

Concetta served everything family-style, and they ate whatever portion they wanted on small plates, which magically disappeared and reappeared as each course changed into the next. She always seemed to be in motion, and yet she was always seated at the head of the table, calmly enjoying the effects of good food on her family. She had impeccable table manners, and the tiniest cough from her would remind her sons to be on their best behavior at the table, too. There was gentle laughter and good-natured storytelling, but her presence alone was enough to prevent an argument between the potentially hotheaded brothers, who disagreed on almost everything from sports to politics to how to bait a hook or paint a house.

By now, Tony's sisters had families of their own, so Mary brought a dessert called pizza fritte (fried dough) and showed up with her son Anthony, in between Tommy and Johnny in age. Her husband, Red, was a contractor who worked seven days a week, so he was rarely there. Jeanne's little boy Eugene was just a toddler, so she kept close tabs on him. Her husband was still in the military, stationed nearby but not near enough to join them. Fran had moved out to California to study opera. Donny came once in a while with his wife, plus their daughter JoAnne and son Donny. John was married and living up in Rhode Island. He and his wife, Sally, had an infant daughter of their own. Grace always felt welcome, but she did start to miss seeing her side of the family, especially when Donny asked how her Uncle Len was doing.

Marion waitressed at a restaurant on Hamilton Avenue called Chouquettes, and even though the food there could never rival Concetta's, Grace decided to spend a little time with her aunt and confidante as soon as possible. As fate would have it, one of her cousins, Ruth, whom Aunt Lily had left behind, had also moved out to another suburb recently and was missing her connection to the family, too. They made arrangements to meet for lunch on Wednesday, and Grace got her next-door neighbor's daughter Carla to babysit Johnny when he came home from school so she could stay until Marion's shift was done.

Ruth was waiting at the bus stop near St. Francis Hospital when Grace got off. She was two years younger, and they had never been very close, but they did have a lot in common and looked forward to spending time together. They made small talk as they walked up Hamilton, across the street from Trenton Central High School, and into the restaurant. Marion breezed by them, carrying four plates on each arm. She smiled at both of them warmly and nodded toward an open booth she had saved for them. They ordered open faced turkey sandwiches with coleslaw, cranberry sauce, mashed potatoes, and gravy. Marion had already told them it was the best thing on the menu.

"Kind of nice to eat something that isn't Italian for a change," Grace admitted cautiously, and Ruth laughed out loud in appreciation for the way she had dispensed with the formalities. They had both married Italian men, both had kids, and both moved to the suburbs. As far as their grandmother or either of their mothers would have been concerned, they had both already hit the jackpot in life. But both of them felt like they were missing something, and it was nice knowing someone else understood.

"Does your husband think he knows everything, too?" Ruth ventured further into common territory, and Grace laughed, thankful hers wasn't the only husband afflicted with overconfidence. As the conversation continued, they talked about their kids, the local schools, and neighborhoods. They were just starting to talk about how much they missed feeling connected to the Knowlton women, when Marion finished her shift and sat down in the booth beside Grace.

"Well, that's simple. We should get the Yackers Club back together again," Marion offered as a matter of fact. They all agreed it was high time somebody called up all the cousins, aunts, and sisters for a meeting. It had been a few years since they had all gotten together. They shared each other's excitement and set about creating a list on the spot.

There were close to thirty names on it, so they decided to split up the calls between them. They picked the last Sunday of the month to give them time to get in touch with everyone. They would also have to explain to their husbands that, from now on, there would be one night a month when they would have to babysit while the women got together. On top of that, Grace had to explain to Tone why the first meeting was going to be at their house.

Surprisingly, Tony thought it was a great idea. In truth, he thought if she could see them all once a month, he wouldn't have to worry about visiting them at all, himself. He liked a few of them, but in small doses, and most of the men felt the same way about each other. They all accepted the monthly meetings, as if they really had a choice, and agreed to attend a party or two throughout the year, reluctantly.

With both sons in school now and Tony still doing shift work, Grace added to the tasks of being a housewife and mom by becoming a den mother for Johnny's Cub Scout troop as well as President of the PTA and the unofficial social secretary of the Yackers Club, too. Apparently, she liked to keep herself busy, and on top of those activities, she had finally started making real friends in the neighborhood, like Jackie and Eileen.

Jackie Bullock lived down the other end of Lowell Avenue and had two sons and a daughter with her husband Ray. Eileen Schipske lived around the corner on Eaton Avenue and had three boys with her husband, Bob. Grace was so close to both of them that she probably would have invited them to join the Yackers Club if it weren't against the rules. Luckily, both of them had families of their own and didn't feel slighted in the least by not being invited to join hers.

On the night of the first Yackers Club meeting ever held on Lowell Avenue, Tony took the boys over to his brother's house in Levittown. As luck would have it, the annual rebroadcast of *The Wizard of Oz* was on television that night, so the kids would be fully entertained, leaving the two brothers alone for a couple of hours. Luckily, Donny's wife Jo joined them to referee the conversation, after making sure the kids had enough ham sandwiches, drinks, pretzels, and potato chips to last throughout the film.

The Yackers Club had a simple set of guidelines that had functioned well for years. The first thing they did was go once around the room for any announcements a member wanted to make. One aunt was expecting a grandchild. Another one's son was getting married. One cousin had just bought a house in yet another suburb. One distant relative had passed away. Next, members volunteered for, or were selected to join, a committee that planned for a holiday party, whether that was Christmas, Halloween, or the Fourth of July. The final order of business was a non-traditional exchange they called a "tricky-tray." Each one of them brought a wrapped gift, usually a kitchen or household item, valued at less than a dollar-fifty. They placed them all in a large basket, which they passed around the room for each member to choose one. Grace had wrapped a couple extra ones for cousins she knew weren't in very good financial shape, so they wouldn't be embarrassed. As they expressed their gratitude for new potato peelers, needle and thread kits, a scented candle, or a wooden spoon, the hostess served coffee and desserts.

Aunt Bessie made sure she got a tour of the house, having never been there before. Aunt Myrtle had brought her two eldest daughters, Diane and Joyce, into the fold. Avah was all grown up now and had a daughter of her own.

Aunt Carrie caught up with Marion, and when her cousin Ruth hugged Grace in the kitchen, she knew her first time as hostess had been a complete success.

Being in touch with her family again brought out the best in Grace. She had more fun with her boys and enjoyed the neighborhood friendships she was developing. She kept busy with arts and crafts for the Cub Scouts and the PTA, but also found time for a night out every now and then with Tony, taking advantage of babysitters in the family, including Aunt Bessie, whom little Johnny nicknamed Bep. Uncle Breck had passed away, and Aunt Bep was happy for the company, although she would never admit it.

"You can sleep on the sofa," she said, pointing Tommy in that direction. "And you can share the bed with me, as long as you keep your guinea hands to yourself," Aunt Bep exclaimed to Grace's youngest, who laughed at everything she said. When he repeated it to Grace the next morning, she knew some things would never change.

Where Tommy had been an average student, in first grade Johnny was already being called "gifted" and "talented." His first grade teacher, Miss Jacqueline Strohauer, was young and very attractive, in a blonde cheerleader kind of way. He was only seven years old, but he fell in love with her when he opened the private bathroom door and saw her sitting there with her thighs exposed above her stockings. Neither of them blushed. She sternly instructed him to close the door behind him and knock before he ever opened it again. The kids had been on the playground and she had forgotten to lock the door. She was a first-year teacher who would not make that mistake again. She told Grace the story after they had become friends through the PTA, and Grace couldn't help but wonder why Johnny had never mentioned it. Although Johnny had managed not to blush during the incident, he blushed when she brought it up, and she wrote it off as his being too embarrassed by the incident to share it.

Johnny was blushing again when his teacher showed up at his house one weekend in tight denim shorts and a white halter top with a bare midriff. Tony was very pleased to meet her and remarked what a great tan she had. She innocently lifted the halter top slightly to reveal a tan line, and twelve-year-old Tommy almost passed out, whispering "hubba hubba," under his breath.

Grace smiled without a hint of jealousy as all three of her boys became smitten with the young vivacious blonde. She had asked Grace for help with a craft project for her Beaver College reunion, and everybody in the house decided to pitch in with the Native American theme. Grace and Miss Strohauer planned to make novelty tomahawks and sell them at the gathering as part of the fundraising efforts. First, Tony and Grace would visit a local turkey farm and grab up all the feathers they could get. They would clean and dye them in a galvanized steel washtub they already had, while Tommy and his best friend Jimmy Clark would collect sticks long and thick enough to serve as hatchet handles. Tony had a friend with a jigsaw come over, and they cut a hundred fake hatchet heads out of balsa wood. The whole family formed an assembly line at the dining room table the following weekend, with their very welcome guest, to cut notches in the sticks, attach the hatchet heads to the handles, and add the dyed turkey feathers for a decorative touch.

Miss Strohauer was delighted with the results and would sell them the next weekend for five dollars each. The kiss on the cheek she gave each of the three Calu boys was all the payment they needed. The hug she gave Grace was like that of a kid sister who couldn't thank her enough. This was 1960, and Grace was an attractive thirty-five-year-old herself, entering a brand new era. There was nothing wrong with watching her husband and her sons appreciate a young, gorgeous visitor, but she did marvel at the lengths to which they all went to please her.

CHAPTER SEVEN

ON APRIL 6, 1960, TOMMY WATCHED his father shadow box his way down the staircase of their humble little Cape Cod into the living room, while proclaiming himself king of his own castle.

"The big four-oh, baby, and I'm better than ever," Tony said. He punched the air, counting in Italian, and thumbed the side of his nose like a prize fighter about to take on whatever life laid in front of him. When the bills were paid and he had an extra twenty in his pocket, Tony was a happy man. He considered himself pretty lucky these days. Sure, the steel mill was a grind, but what job wasn't? Grace kept a nice home for them, and there was always food in the fridge. His boys were both healthy and doing well in school. They had a bright future ahead of them. Who knew, maybe one of them would grow up to become the lawyer he had always wanted to be.

The weather was nice enough for a little yard work, and he had the day off. Shift work had its perks, and so did his position as a security guard. One night, he got to talking with a co-worker at the mill and found out U.S. Steel was going to plant a show-stopping garden to disprove any notions of them polluting the area. As luck would have it, the groundskeeper wasn't averse to making an extra buck, so he discreetly sold twenty-pound bags of ammonium nitrate to those few guys who knew what to do with a top-notch fertilizer. Three bags found their way into Tony's trunk, and he couldn't wait to spread them all over his lawn and garden. He swore his wife and kids to secrecy.

"Italian gardener, my ass," he told Tommy, explaining it was all about the nitrogen. "They're gonna wonder what the hell my secret is by the time summer rolls around." He never actually showed Tommy how to take care of a lawn or plant a garden, but he talked him through it while he did it. In his mind, Tommy was going to make enough money someday to hire a gardener, and another guy to change the oil in his car, while he handled the paperwork for guys even richer than him.

That's the way the world worked as far as he could tell. His father had been a stonemason and busted his back to put food on the table for his kids. Most of them had landed jobs that didn't require much physical labor, and they expected their kids to land jobs that wouldn't require any. Hell, automation was coming anyway. They might as well learn what they needed to get into management. There were a few guys in the neighborhood who had already made that leap a generation earlier for their families. Nort Parker was some kind of stockbroker or something like that. Rockell was a school teacher. Carl, next door, was an architect. That Alito guy around the corner dressed pretty nice. He was either some kind of businessman or a lawyer. His kid even carried a briefcase at ten years old, but other than them, most of the Italians in the neighborhood were barely tolerated. They were okay as long as they didn't throw any loud parties and took good care of their lawns. "Well," Tony laughed to himself, "I'll show them how to take good care of a lawn, alright."

Between cooking, housework, the occasional sewing job, and serving on the PTA, Grace kept herself pretty busy. Her childhood had taught her you had to work hard for whatever you wanted in life, and she wasn't about to let an opportunity slip by when it presented itself. One day, she was shopping around the corner from home at Tracy's Five and Dime, when another customer thought she worked there and asked if she knew where to find a button like one she held in her hand. Without hesitation, Grace led her to another aisle and helped her find a match. The store manager watched it happen and asked her if she was interested in a part-time job. She negotiated the hours she wanted and more money than originally offered to start the following week. Now all she had to do was tell Tony, the king of his castle.

She served him one of his favorite dinners, roast beef with gravy, mashed potatoes, and succotash, then let the kids go outside to play when they finished. She cleared the table and watched Tony lean back and light a cigarette before she broke the news.

He felt like he had been sucker punched.

"What the hell do you want to go and do that for? I make enough money to take care of whatever we need!" It wasn't a matter of need, she explained, sitting down so she could face him eye to eye. It was a matter of opportunity. She gave him a smile and a playful grin. It was right around the corner and only a few hours a day. It wouldn't get in the way of her housework or the cooking or anything else. She reached out and gently put her hand on his. She could save up money for Christmas or help out with summer vacation.

"I don't want no goddamned TV dinners, Grace," he said softly as he gave in reluctantly. She promised it would never come to that. He cut her off when she started to tell him how much she was going to get paid.

"I don't want to hear about it. That's your money, and you do whatever you want with it. I pay the bills around here, and you don't *have* to go to work. I won't stop you, but it better not get in the way of taking care of me and the boys. Are we clear on that?" He already regretted it, but he knew her well enough to know she was going to end up doing it anyway. She gave him a kiss on the cheek, which he thought of as consolation for having lost his first battle in the war of the sexes.

A few weeks later, Grace was in the basement, sewing an outfit for one of her aunts, when she let out a scream that shook the house. Tommy was the first one downstairs, but he turned a ghostly white and ran up to get his father, who was sleeping after a double shift at the mill. In the meantime, little Johnny went down to see his mother and stared, uncomprehending, at the needle that had gone into his mother's fingernail and all the way through her finger. She smiled bravely at him through the tears in her eyes and told him to go back upstairs. Everything would be fine, she said. Tony came down and slowly reversed the needle, wrapping her bleeding finger in his handkerchief and leading her out to the car, while calmly instructing Tommy to look after his younger brother while he took their mother to the hospital.

When everything was indeed fine, the finger bandaged and the throbbing finally subsided, Tony made a point of telling her he blamed it all on her part-time job. If she hadn't been so busy all the time, she wouldn't have been rushing to finish what she was sewing, and this never would have happened. She didn't know if he really believed that, but she wasn't going to let him get away with playing her knight in shining armor on one hand, while he tried to be her jailer on the other. This was an accident that could have happened at any time to anyone. She enjoyed being out of the house, even if it was only a few hours a day, and no one was going to take that away from her.

That next week, Tony and the boys ate their first Swanson-brand Salisbury steak TV dinners while Grace was out at a PTA meeting. The boys thought it was great. Tony kept his opinion to himself and drank an extra couple of beers that night.

Dwight D. Eisenhower had completed the interstate roadway before he left office in January, and now John F. Kennedy challenged the nation to land a man on the moon before the end of the decade. All Tony Calu wanted was a home-cooked meal and a chance to go surf fishing with his kid brother. When Grace got home that night, her husband was already sound asleep and snoring like hell. She counted that among her blessings. Rather than battle it out, they didn't talk much the rest of that month and avoided each other as much as they could, since neither knew what the other was thinking.

Tony thought the answer was money. He heard the YMCA was looking for a swimming instructor to give lessons at local pools that summer, so, having been a lifeguard right after he left the service, he applied for and got the position. He also lined up a part-time job driving school buses in the fall so he could keep more cash coming in. He told Grace she wouldn't have to work anymore now, since he was going to bring in extra money. He had a hard time understanding her reaction.

"Tony, do you really have to work three jobs?"

"C'mon Gracie, what the hell do you want from me? I thought this would make you happy."

"I *am* happy, Tony, but it's not all about the money. I just wanted to pitch in so we could spend a whole week together, as a family, in Seaside this summer. We could lie on the beach every day, eat hot dogs and French fries on the boardwalk at night, and drink lemonade. You could even take the boys fishing."

She painted a pretty picture. It caught him off-guard.

"Well, why the hell didn't you say so, honey? That sounds great! Let's do it!"

Grace kept working at the five and dime, and Tony took the boys with him while he taught hundreds of kids how to swim at pools all around the neighborhood in the early months of summer. They saved up enough money for the last two weeks in August at the Jersey Shore and took Aunt Bessie with them. Each of the boys took a neighborhood friend, too, and the place they rented from the Hoffman's on Franklin Street was crowded and noisy but full of fun for every one of them.

When the boys went back to school, Grace was happy for a little time alone. She didn't even mind when Tony decided to spend the rest of his available vacation days in Rhode Island, fishing with his kid brother. She would have preferred having him home for their anniversary, but that was the only time his brother could get off, and besides, the striped bass were supposed to be running, so she kissed him goodbye and looked forward to a little quiet reading time.

She couldn't go very far without a car. Tony promised to teach her how to drive next year, and she started saving up for a car of her own, but since she could walk to work and was close enough to the grocery store, she didn't mind the fresh air and exercise. If she wanted to visit Marion, she could always hop a bus to Trenton. It used to feel strange when they first got there, being all the way out in the suburbs, but by now the neighborhood was filled with young couples and growing families, so businesses were following them out of the city.

There was a brand new shopping center opening up a couple blocks away on Route 33, so Grace and Jackie Bullock decided to take a walk together and see what shops were opening up. Jackie's youngest son, Timmy, was a year younger than Grace's Johnny and had just started kindergarten, so she finally had a free morning to herself, as well. They laughed like schoolgirls away from their husbands and children.

When Grace saw the magazine rack at Thrift Drugs, she knew she was going to enjoy her time alone while Tone was gone fishing. She picked up the latest issues of *Life*, *Glamour*, *Good Housekeeping,* and *Reader's Digest*. Jackie picked up a copy of *Field and Stream*, mentioning that her husband Ray liked to fish, too, but he preferred going out on a boat, while Tony liked to cast from the surf.

"Well, let's not get them started together, or we'll never see them," Grace responded to the news, to which Jackie replied, "You say that like it's a bad thing," and they both laughed cautiously. Luckily, they each had a good marriage and could joke about their men without being misunderstood. They both knew there was more than one woman in the neighborhood who didn't have it so good.

"Boys will be boys" had turned into "men will be men," and while all the latest magazines were chock-full of articles on how to keep your man happy at home or how to do wonders with leftover chicken, the dashing new young president had just told reporters he was enjoying Ian Fleming's book about James Bond, the ultimate spy, womanizer, and man's man.

Over a cup of coffee back at Jackie's house on her way home, Grace admitted that Tony had voted for Nixon. Even though he was Catholic, he didn't trust the handsome young Irish New Englander and son of a bootlegger. Ray didn't like him either, but Jackie was more interested in his wife. After all, they shared a name, and who didn't love her sense of fashion? Both women agreed, identifying with the Lady of Camelot.

The rest of the week was sheer fun. Norman Vincent Peale inspired Grace with the power of positive thinking in an excerpt from *Reader's Digest*. People had always told her she looked like Elizabeth Taylor, who stared at her from the cover of *Life* magazine, so she decided to make a Cleopatra costume for the Yackers Club Halloween party. She found out that the kids loved chicken à la king over toast, and that gave her two meals for every chicken she cooked. She decided she was a little too old for a miniskirt, but not bad for a mother of two. She welcomed Tony home as a woman confident in her own appeal. He thought maybe he should go away a little more often.

CHAPTER EIGHT

JOHNNY PLAYED CAPTAIN HOOK in a class production of "Peter Pan." The U.S. President took a fatal bullet in Dallas, and fall gave way to winter. The nation was in a state of shock, but mourning would not deter Madison Avenue from making the most of Christmas.

Tony had put in a lot of overtime that year in order to place a bongo board and transistor radio underneath the white aluminum tree lit by a spinning color wheel, not to mention the big surprise, which was a brand new regulation-size pool table he had somehow managed to get down into the basement while the kids were in school. Grace cooked a holiday feast, and it seemed the celebration went right on through New Year's Eve, with friends and family stopping by to eat and play, laugh and drink, making the most of the season.

Aunt Jeanne's young son Eugene threw a dart that somehow struck a pipe and sprung a leak, but Tony taped it quickly. Everybody laughed about it, but Jeanne was mortified. By this time the poor woman was widowed and living with her mom again, more dependent than ever on her approval. Concetta was gentle by nature, but harder on her daughters than she was on her sons. It was the only way she knew how to prepare them for whatever came in life. Mothers were hard on their daughters and fathers were hard on their sons.

Tony was no exception to that rule. He treated his first born the way he had been treated and expected complete obedience. Tommy was a bit shy as an adolescent, and that was only exacerbated by the shadow of a father who was larger than life. Those few times he did try to stand up for himself were greeted with a physical reminder of his place at the end of a belt. One particular incident pushed the family to the brink. It was a typical dinner with all four of them at the table, when Tone started to tell a story about his childhood. They had all heard it many times before, but only Tommy dared to say something about it.

"You've already told that story too many times!" If he had stopped there, he might have saved himself, but he misjudged his father's slightly baffled reaction and continued. "If I have to hear it one more time, I'm gonna throw this glass of milk in your face!"

Tony raised an eyebrow and continued to tell his story. Tommy threw an entire glass of milk right in his father's face. The eldest son stopped laughing when he saw the lower lip start to tremble and took in the weight of his father's slowly building rage. Tony burst out of his seat and hauled his challenger upstairs by the back of his neck. The two-tongued strap he wielded to his son's bare ass for the next fifteen minutes left a lasting impression and a teenager who wouldn't sit without a pillow for several weeks. Grace was horrified and did her best to comfort her son, who was almost as embarrassed by her attention as he was in pain from his father's.

"What on Earth made you do that?" she asked as she handed him a tissue for the tears he had refused to shed while his father beat him. He muttered something about standing up for himself and then somehow instinctively straightened up for what he knew he had to do next. He acted as if it were a ritual he understood and moved silently downstairs to face his father, who was seated again at the head of the dining room table.

"I'm sorry, Dad." He looked him right in the eye.

Tony had barely calmed down, but dismissed him with what sounded like a low rumbling growl between clenched teeth. When he looked up, Grace was standing there beside her son, staring at her husband fearlessly and with complete disgust.

She waited until both children had left the room to deliver her opinion. "I thought you were a better man than that." She shook her head, sadly, then turned her back on him and walked away.

Both kids walked around on eggshells while the distance between their parents grew. After a silent dinner, Tony would retreat to his basement workshop, where he had stashed a few copies of *Playboy*. He smoked, drank, and read his magazines whenever he was home. Grace stayed out of the basement and spent most of her time reading or planning meals in the kitchen. The only time they spent together was for a grocery shopping trip on payday, every other Saturday.

While they went out to the baker, the butcher, an Italian specialty shop, and the supermarket, Tommy would babysit his brother with a little help from Tarzan or the Bowery Boys. They would feast on fresh rolls and lunch meat with potato chips and cheese pretzels. They would wash it down with ShopRite lemon-lime sodas and have ice cream sandwiches for dessert. In between courses, they would wrestle around the living room watching Leo Gorcey or the Marx Brothers get in and out of trouble. The Lone Ranger shot straight and Superman was everybody's hero. Over time, the peace of their home was restored as Tom became his little brother's protector and their parents did a thorough spring cleaning both inside and outside the house.

Tony's lawn was greener than anybody else's, so when they weren't playing stickball in back of the Bell Telephone building, Johnny played wiffle ball in his own backyard with Johnny Parker and Timmy Bullock from down the street, Randy Rockell from across the street, and Carl "Skipper" Karlberg, Lillian and Carl's second child from next door. Tony joined them one time to even up the sides, remarking that he grew up with a pet Dalmatian named Skipper, to which the neighbor's kid responded by barking enthusiastically.

Meanwhile, Tommy had started playing third base in Babe Ruth League and was building a reputation as a solid hitter. His uncle Donny gave him a ball autographed by an old friend, Willie Mays, who used to play for the Trenton Giants in the negro league, back when Donny was known around town as a top-notch amateur boxer. Willie played center field for the San Francisco Giants now, so they automatically became Tommy and Johnny's favorite team from then on. They never did get to meet him, but they told everybody they had. When Jackie told Grace what Johnny had told Timmy, she warned him about telling tall tales and apologized for his overactive imagination, even though she had a soft spot for it and encouraged him in writing his stories.

Tommy on the other hand, was all business. When he heard that Gino Marchetti, a famous football player, was opening up a chain of fast food restaurants, he was the first one in line to apply for a job. He worked full-time all summer, slinging hamburgers and French fries just to make sure he had the afterschool shifts for the fall.

While Tommy did grill duty and Grace took a new job over at Thrift Drugs because it paid more than the five and dime, Tony took Johnny with him to a few different neighborhood pools that summer, to continue his role as a swimming instructor for the Y. Johnny was little, but he knew how to swim and kept tabs on the bigger kids as if he were a junior lifeguard. Tony was tan and handsome in his black bathing suit, with a hairy chest and a whistle around his neck on a braided plastic chain that Tommy had made in the Boy Scouts. All the young mothers who brought their kids for lessons enjoyed watching him strut his stuff along the edges of the pool. He rarely got in the water, but when he did, it was by way of a perfect jackknife off the side of the pool and you could almost hear the sighs as he slicked his hair back before stepping up out of the water on a shiny silver ladder.

One of Grace's girlfriends from the PTA, who happened to live close to one of the pools where Tony was teaching, warned her that she had better keep a close eye on him. She grudgingly joined that friend for lunch one day and dropped by to see what all the fuss was about. She was surprised how it made her feel. He really did look good, all tan and lean, and every woman in the crowd actually did have their eyes on him. It was a little unsettling, and she was feeling self-conscious, as if some of these women saw her as a rival. When one of them casually remarked how lucky she was, she replied that not everything was as good as it looked. She immediately regretted her response and decided not to make matters worse by hanging around. She went home and whipped up one of her best meals, before sprucing up a little more than usual, in time to serve Tony dinner. He noticed she was wearing lipstick and wondered if she had on a new dress, too. She played it off as if he were being silly, but that night he asked her to get a sitter for next Saturday, so he could take her out somewhere nice.

Landwehr's was somewhere nice, and Grace was happy to be there. Even though she had used her feminine wiles to convince her husband to take her out, she hadn't expected anything this fancy. Tony had casually asked Carl next door for a recommendation, figuring any guy who wore a tuxedo as often as he did should know someplace nicer than the run of the mill. This place was up on River Road and oozed charm the minute they walked in the door. He was glad Carl had told him to make a reservation. He would have felt like a fool without one. The *maître d'* showed them to their table, and he ordered whiskey sours as a jazz trio played softly nearby. The food was delicious, if a bit pricey, and it felt almost like a second honeymoon. When Tony asked her to dance, he erased all the distance fifteen years had created between them. While they were out on the dance floor, a woman dancing beside them recognized her son's swimming instructor.

"Tony? Is that you? My goodness, you dance just as well as you swim," she gushed, only slightly inebriated. He didn't know who she was and had no interest in finding out, but her husband insisted on buying a round of drinks while they got to know each other.

"What line of work are you in, Tony?"

"Oh my, that's a lovely dress. Grace, isn't it?"

This couple was adept at social banter, but they obviously couldn't tell Tony and Grace would rather have been left alone. Tony was also from the school of thought that wouldn't let anyone buy him a drink without reciprocating, so they had to stay for round two. They handled it the best they could and were almost ready to leave when Grace spotted Eileen and Bob from the neighborhood and excused herself to greet them.

The Schipskes were celebrating their anniversary. They lived on Eaton Avenue, around the corner from Jackie and Ray. They had a son Tommy's age, one two years older than Johnny, and one two years younger. Eileen and Grace were already good friends, but their husbands had never spent any time together. Grace saw a chance to make that happen and took it.

"Are you two half as uncomfortable here as we are? Do you feel like stopping by our place for coffee?" The look of relief on their faces matched the look on Tony's when all three of them went over to collect him.

Bob worked for the post office and Eileen worked at Dunham's, of all places. The four of them hit it off effortlessly. While Grace and Eileen talked about the fashionable ladies of Landwehr's and the quality of dresses from Macy's and Bamberger's, Tony and Bob found common ground in yard work and politics, craftsmanship and statesmanship, plus respect for a good automobile. In no time, the four had made plans for another night out together, with both men suggesting they find someplace a little more reasonably priced this time.

By the time that summer ended, the two couples had gone out to dinner and the movies together, spent a day at the beach, and had a picnic in Grace and Tony's backyard. Their kids got along well, too, and in short order the neighborhood friendships included the Bullocks, the Bankers, and the Baras from a few blocks away. They started a penny ante poker night once a month, rotating to each other's houses. The ladies concentrated on finger sandwiches, chips, and dips, while the men drank each other's beer. They gossiped about their neighbors and kibitzed about suburban life in general. The big winner of the night might take home a dollar-fifty, and the biggest loser might have lost half of that. Their homes were built and furnished alike. Their kids went to the same schools. They all had to work for a living, and none of them took themselves too seriously. Tony grew the best tomatoes. George and Peggy Banker canned sweet pickles. Grace hemmed dresses for Madge Bara and her two daughters.

Bob helped Tony change the oil in his car. Ray and Tony kept their two oldest sons from duking it out. Jackie and Eileen both tried to convince Grace she should go back to work full time. They all became the best friends any of them had ever had.

That fall, Johnny played Macbeth in a school production of the Shakespeare classic and fell in love with his Lady Macbeth. Out, damned spot, he knew her lines and spent all his time memorizing sonnets that weren't even in the play. Grace knew he was smitten and told her husband he was much too young for that, but Tony refused to talk about it. He figured his kid had a hundred crushes ahead of him. He just hoped he would grow out of his theatrical nonsense.

Tommy was another story. He did his best to avoid any drama. He developed a small circle of friends, taught his little brother how to play pool well enough to beat most of them for money, and maintained an uneasy detente with his father. Whereas Tony was a fly-by-the-seat-of-his-pants kind of guy, his oldest son became a careful planner. Tommy saved most of what he made at Gino's, and thanks to the encouragement of one particular teacher, he started to see himself as college-bound, with the potential for a career in business. He kept it to himself and confided only in his mother, who cautioned him as much as she supported him, recognizing the limits of their ability to help him financially. Theirs was a candid, protective, and always honest relationship. They both knew they would do anything for each other and both accepted that it never needed to be said. She admired his growing strength of character, and he confided in her freely, appreciating the respect she showed him for the privacy of his thoughts.

There was a certain point in time when Tony felt like he was losing control of his home. Grace was working more hours at the drugstore than he wanted her to and spending lots of time with her girlfriends. He was eating at least one frozen dinner and one takeout meal every damned week. Tommy behaved himself well enough but never had anything to talk about with his old man. Little Johnny's head was somewhere in the clouds, singing and writing plays or talking about how Jesus would have hated the Catholic Church for the hypocrisy of the priests and parishioners. Where the hell did he get ideas like that? It was only spring, but Tony couldn't wait for another summer vacation at the shore. Luckily, he didn't have to wait that long for some much-needed excitement. An old army buddy called him up out of the blue to tell him that his troop was having a reunion in New York City. It was music to his ears and just what the doctor ordered.

Grace didn't know much about her husband's time in the service. He had been stationed down in Trinidad and Tobago, worked on billeting troops as they were transported overseas. Even though he hadn't been in combat himself, he had lost friends and didn't like to talk about it much. As far as she could gather, he gambled and drank his way through World War II, but didn't believe in whoring it up, out of fear of syphilis, as well as the condemnation he would have faced from his family and the Holy Roman Catholic Church. She figured one weekend in New York wouldn't kill him, so she was fine with the reunion, not that he had asked for her opinion or permission, anyway.

While Grace and her sons went about their regular routine for a Thursday and Friday, Tony took a train to New York and rolled the dice – literally, rolled the dice. Enjoying the camaraderie in a fine hotel, with aged prime steaks and top-shelf booze, he had such an extraordinary streak of good luck that he ended up taking a taxi cab home all the way from New York City on Saturday morning. He was still drunk when he arrived. He tipped the driver a hundred-dollar bill and tripped through the front door, laughing as he landed on the living room floor, shouting for his family to join him in his merriment. They would never forget the smile on his face or the image of the rascal who greeted them, with five-, ten-, and twenty-dollar bills spilling out of every single pocket of his shirt, pants, and jacket.

"Anybody want to help me count this stuff?" he laughed, rolling over on his winnings and pulling more out of his socks and shoes. He had seventeen hundred forty-three dollars left, after covering the last night's bar tab for the whole troop, settling up his own hotel bill, including a room service breakfast he couldn't remember, and tipping his taxi driver lavishly. Needless to say, his mood was greatly improved, and the feeling would last all summer, even if the money didn't. They put a little away for the summer vacation. They put some away for a rainy day. They helped out a cousin with a kid in trouble. They bought themselves new furniture, and then the luck ran out.

Little Johnny had a bad stomach ache on their summer vacation and had to be rushed to the hospital for an emergency appendectomy. Tony's old car needed new tires. The Frigidaire stop working, so they had to get it fixed. That's as far as the dice had rolled.

When Tony went back to work after Labor Day, he was passed over for a promotion he felt he deserved. The younger gentleman who got the job happened to be black, and though Tony wasn't particularly racist, he clearly felt he was the victim of reverse discrimination and didn't keep it to himself at home. He mainly complained about this one "stupid-ass black man," but the issue of color was all over the news, and his family knew where he stood. Little by little, Tony came to hate his job. Grace wasn't enjoying hers that much, either, and Eileen told her about an opening at Dunham's new Lawrenceville store. That meant working a couple nights a week, but the boys were old enough to look after themselves now. Tony was dead set against it and yet helpless to prevent it. They argued about it until he gave in, not that she had asked for his permission, anyway.

The neighborhood was rapidly changing. One poor couple couldn't keep their private lives a secret, and everybody knew the wife was on a barstool by herself most weekend nights. Another poor guy lost his marbles and was rumored to have run naked down the middle of the street at midnight, shouting out that life had too many options. "Too many options!" The first neighborhood teen died over in Vietnam. They built a private swimming club a few blocks away on Elmore Avenue, and it became very clear that less than half the people in the neighborhood could afford to belong. The Karlbergs finally did get a chance to move to a bigger house, but instead of Princeton, where Lillian would have preferred, it was right down the street, less than a block away. Their son, Skipper, started having problems in school, and the other kids started to avoid him. Carla was away at college by then and not likely to return if she could avoid it.

The first time his sons had ever seen him cry was the day his mother died. Tony put on a brave face, but he knew it was the end of an era. Without Concetta's Sunday dinners, the brothers and sisters wouldn't spend much time together anymore. They still made an effort to stay in touch, but time has a way of distancing those who allow it to. Grace did her best to stay in touch with Tony's family, while she relied on the Yackers Club to stay in touch with hers.

If Tony had become distant from his brothers and sisters, he had become nonexistent to Grace's uncles, aunts, and cousins. He wanted nothing to do with any of them and made no secret of it. The loss of his mother, plus his dissatisfaction at work, had narrowed his family and social life down to his wife and kids, Bob Schipske, who he still got along with, plus one fellow bus driver and fishing buddy named Jack, who took the October trips up to Rhode Island with him to visit his kid brother. Other than those connections and a few outings with them, Grace had to drag him anywhere she wanted to go. Once he got there, he was still the life of the party, but she was exhausted by the effort it took to get him there. Over time, it just got easier for her to go by herself, and she did.

Grace, Eileen, Jackie, Madge, and Peggy from the poker games added Sadie and Ginny from the neighborhood for a variety of exciting excursions to Atlantic City, The Smithville Inn, and even New York City. They took a car ride, a bus trip, or a train trip every other month. They went to Broadway shows and craft villages, pageants and parades. They dined in modestly upscale restaurants and dressed up to enjoy the occasions. Every single one of them looked forward to their adventures, and not a single husband ever realized how important it was to them. The husbands only joined them for an occasional poker night and the obligatory New Year's Eve Party.

Happy New Year! Grace lit a cigarette once a year. She had become a mild smoker after meeting Tony, but a doctor mentioned they had a potentially harmful effect on her baby when she was pregnant with Tom and she quit on the spot. She often wished Tony would think about quitting. Aside from the health risks everybody was starting to talk about, she was sick of the smell, but on New Year's Eve, she forgot about it for a night and celebrated alongside him. They dressed up in their finest once a year, dined upscale with friends they enjoyed, and danced like they were Fred Astaire and Ginger Rogers. She cried every time she heard

Auld Lang Syne, identifying it with the mother she lost and the father she never knew.

A few months later, the health risks caught up with him. Tony was hospitalized and operated on for bleeding ulcers. They removed a third of his stomach and left a large scar in the shape of a question mark down the middle of his chest. Luckily, his Blue Cross and Blue Shield covered the cost of the operation, but the reduced income from his lack of overtime and the missing money that used to come in from side jobs made Grace realize just how hard the poor guy worked to provide the life they had. Tommy tried to pitch in with the paycheck from his part-time job, but his parents would never accept it. Tate Anderson, their favorite butcher, actually came to visit Tony and told him that his credit was always good for whatever he needed. That was an act of kindness they never expected and would never forget.

Things were pretty tight for a while until he got back on his feet, but the boys barely noticed other than the fact that Eileen, Jackie, Aunt Marion, Aunt Carrie, Avah, and Tony's sisters seemed to show up with a casserole every other day for several months. In times of trouble, the people who love you bring food. In times of struggle, the people who care will share.

Tony was somewhat humbled by his illness. He did not like having to depend on anyone, but he genuinely appreciated those who had come to the aid of his wife and sons. He might never have started smoking again if his family physician hadn't lit one up in front of him and casually suggested it was okay for him to have one, too, now that the surgery was over. Grace could have killed the guy with her bare hands, but Tony took his word for gospel and was back to a pack a day in no time. His drinking and antisocial sentiments came back with a vengeance, too, when he found the situation at work no more tolerable than it had been before he was sidelined.

Johnny managed to make it through Confirmation that spring with Uncle Len standing as his proud sponsor, before he told his father he would not be going to church anymore. They were starting to say the mass in English now and singing folk songs in the middle of the service, so while Tony put up a fight, he was actually kind of relieved not to have to attend. Tommy's work schedule had excused him from going for the past couple of years, so he quietly slipped away without a fuss. Tony was tired of arguing with his youngest son about goodness and the saints and forgiveness for sinners. He just wanted to pray somewhere quietly in peace, so he started going to an early morning mass still held in Latin and attended by old-timers who didn't want the church to change. Tony had seen a little too much change lately, and the church was a bridge too far. He prayed for some way to escape his self-imposed exile, bored with his job and convinced that there was more to life than a steady job and a suburban home. He tinkered with clothespins in his basement workshop, trying to invent a better mousetrap or anything else he could sell. He tended his garden but lost touch with his seeds and drank himself silly, ignoring his wife's needs.

It took his oldest son's graduation to snap him out of his rut. He and Grace stood proudly beside Tommy in his flowing green gown. They were delighted when he told them he had been accepted at Rider College. That would guarantee him a deferment, and nobody was happier than Grace to keep her son away from Vietnam. Tony started to envision the kind of wonderful future his son could have once he graduated from this prestigious business school. He became his son's adviser while Grace remained her son's confidante. All of a sudden, they had plenty to talk about and a million more things in common than they had ever realized before. Tony helped Tommy grow out of his shell, and Tommy pulled Tony out of his basement, all to Grace's sheer happiness. She had always known they were more alike than they realized. It was about time they started to see it, too.

Over the next few years, Johnny joined a folk rock group with one of the Schipskes' sons. The Alito kid around the corner got accepted at Princeton. Grace left Dunham's for a job closer to home at the Motor Club of America. Tony didn't care for the way the insurance agents looked at his wife. The Yackers Club held a summer picnic and the Bullocks got a Cadillac. Grace sewed a flower girl dress for one of Avah's kids, and we landed a man on the moon. Johnny shot pool at Sam "the Plumber" DeCavalcante's house, and Grace listened to Jimi Hendrix's "Are You Experienced" but liked James Taylor better.

Tone tried to teach Johnny how to drive in a Ford Falcon with a stick shift on the column, over a steep black bridge known for traffic jams. Tom, who had joined the TKE Fraternity and become a big man on campus, came to his kid brother's rescue by showing him how to drive a cool Dodge Dart with black bucket seats and a push-button automatic transmission.

The first day he had his driver's license, Johnny drove his mother downtown to Sears with two of his friends in the backseat of her Chevy Malibu. The parking lot was crowded, and he misjudged a space as he tried to enter. Nervous at the cars moving behind him, he stepped on the gas instead of the brake and slid a two-foot long scratch on the door of the car beside him. His mother got out and negotiated a cash settlement with the startled driver, shaking her head at her son, whom she left in the car while she went in to pick up an item she'd ordered. He wouldn't drive again for the next few months, and then, when he finally did, his girlfriend left a little menstrual blood on the backseat of that same Chevy Malibu when they got caught in the rain and decided to finish their fun in the car. Grace couldn't figure out what she did to deserve such disrespect, and she was not shy in letting him know. Like she had done with his older brother, she kept their conversations and awkward incidents confidential between them, but this one was testing her limits.

He was testing his own limits, too. Johnny had always been popular, but for the first time in his life, he wondered why – and if it mattered at all. Young men were dying in Vietnam. Presidents and spiritual leaders could be assassinated. The military industrial complex only cared about turning kids like him into consumers. That was the kind of angst he carried with him and couldn't seem to drown out, no matter how hard he tried.

When he came home late from a party one night, his father was on the night shift and his brother was up at the frat house. His mom heard him come in and asked him how the party was. In true dramatic teenage fashion, he told her that his life wasn't worth living anymore. He just wished he could go to sleep and not wake up again. He heard her crying across the hall before she gently knocked on his door and asked if she could come in.

That night, Grace poured out the details of her father's suicide, heart to heart, in a way her son could not ignore. She described how she had overcome the struggles and insecurity of her childhood with a little help from Norman Vincent Peale, birds in flight, the smell of the ocean, and the sound of a piano.

"I don't know where I heard it first, but before we're born, we're afraid to leave the womb, since everything we need is taken care of. Once we're born, we find out there is so much more than we could ever have imagined. It's not all good and not all bad. It's just more, and it's up to us to make the best of it. When we die, I think it's the same thing. Not necessarily good or bad. Just more, and up to us to make the best of it, but please don't be in a hurry. There are some pretty amazing things to see and do while you're here."

With that, she kissed him on the forehead and left him to make sense of what she'd shared.

CHAPTER NINE

HE WAS A LITTLE IMMATURE, but he was the first one she saw this spring and it filled her with joy. Grace had a deep connection to the Northern Cardinals that landed in her backyard every year about this time. Her association was personal and visceral, not born of any reading or mythology. The young male was a pale red with mottled feathers and a ruffled appearance. He reminded her of someone she knew. As a knowing smile spread across her face, a full-grown male with a clearly defined black mask, in striking contrast to its brilliant red plumage, landed right beside what might have been his son.

She sat enjoying her morning coffee on the screened-in back porch that Tony had built with their own immature progeny at the end of the previous summer. Father and sons had fought like cats and dogs in the process, each shouting at the other to hold the boards steady or measure them twice before cutting. It was incredible that the end product had as few defects as it did, and a good coat of paint covered up most of them. The one thing Tony always had right was to use good materials. The boys were rightfully proud of what the three of them had built together.

Tony was working the day shift. Johnny had already left for school. Tommy had slept at the frat house again, and Grace didn't have to be at work for another hour and a half. The insurance company was a ten-minute walk from home at most, so she relaxed and enjoyed the peace and quiet of an empty house. Strolling back into the kitchen with her empty coffee cup, she liked what she saw. It was nice and clean, not spotless, but not bad either. She had sewn the short sunflower-covered curtains for the window overlooking Tony's truck garden. They matched the pot holders hanging on the wall beside the stove. The small Formica table and chairs were still in good shape and there was nothing wrong with the red brick linoleum floor, but Tony said he wanted to replace the painted ceiling with tiles next year.

Through the doorway into the dining room, she admired the large and highly polished cherry wood table and chairs. It was a prized possession and she took special care of it, even teaching her youngest son how to dust and polish it whenever company was expected. There was a matching sideboard with plenty of drawer space, but she had tried unsuccessfully for years to get Tony to buy her a couple of nice corner cabinets to complete the room. She could see it in her mind and was determined to have her dream dining room. Not that they entertained all that much anymore, but it was a source of pride and reminded her how far she had come from her boarding house childhood.

She walked through an archway into their less-than-contemporary living room. It was comfortable enough; the upholstered sofa with a matching chair and recliner were accompanied by a coffee table and two end tables, which all faced a small television, next to a cabinet holding a record player, radio, and liquor closet. There were family photos on the wall and a stand full of TV trays for times when the whole family wasn't there to use the dining room. There, Grace enjoyed her favorite afternoon soap operas, *Another World* and *Days of Our Lives*, but usually left the room for the boys while she went to sew in the basement or read in her bedroom most evenings.

As she headed upstairs to get dressed for work, the bathroom was right in front of her. It was small for four people, and she wished she could get Tony to stop smoking in there, because the smell just never went away. She even showed him how nicotine had stained the paneled walls when she wiped them down each week, but he was too stubborn or too addicted to stop.

Their bedroom was the smaller one to the left, and the boys' room was the larger one to the right. Her closet was small, but Tony kept everything except his work uniforms, which he had dry cleaned, in a tall dresser, so she had most of it to herself. She picked out a nice green checkered dress for today with black stockings and heels to match. She liked getting dressed up and putting on lipstick. She didn't particularly like the way one of the agents looked at her, so she was careful not to show any cleavage, even though she was well endowed. She brushed her hair and put on a touch of rouge, kissed a tissue to soften her lipstick, and winked at herself in the mirror before she headed downstairs. If Tony could do it, why couldn't she?

When she walked out the front door that damned Blackie was there. The Karlbergs had moved down the street, but they must have forgotten to tell their cat. Grace had chased him with a broom and even turned a hose on him from Tony's garden, but nothing could keep him away from climbing on top of and underneath their long and otherwise lovely front porch. She hated him as much as she loved the birds in her backyard and could never explain why. They hissed at each other since she didn't have time to chase him this morning.

Her heels clicked down the quiet street as she walked two blocks away and crossed Route 33 to enter a small office building. The girls greeted her warmly, one man whistled his approval, and the owner of the agency said "good morning" politely before closing his office door. She was the primary filing clerk and front counter girl, but she also answered phones and typed up memos when they needed her to pitch in. She spent most of the day on her feet but enjoyed the interaction with customers and coworkers. The days went by quickly, but she was happy to get out of her heels by the end of them. One ass made a pass at her at an office party one time, and she had to ignore a number of off-color comments, but by and large it was a polite business atmosphere, and the man in charge was a decent boss. Tony may not have trusted him, but he never gave Grace any reason to feel uncomfortable.

She made it home in time to have dinner ready for her husband. It would just be the two of them tonight, so they'd eat in the kitchen. Tommy had called to say he wouldn't be home until later, and Johnny had rehearsal for another school play.

Tony was starved, so he sat down and ate in his uniform, after taking off the black knit tie. Minute steak sandwiches with fried onions and canned mushrooms, French fries, and a can of Schmidt's beer put him in a good mood. He had the next couple of days off and was going to take Tommy to Island Beach State Park for a day of surf fishing, so life was good as far as he was concerned.

"Tommy's coming home tonight, right?" Tony asked with genuine concern, adding that they were going fishing in the morning, as if he hadn't already told Grace about it several times. She assured him his eldest son was just as excited about the trip as he was and then carefully brought up her concerns about their younger son.

"I'm a little worried about Johnny," she admitted reluctantly.

She was pretty sure he would outgrow his teenage angst, but she didn't want to be the only one he could confide in. She had already made that mistake with her oldest son. Tommy and his father were getting along well now, but they still couldn't talk about anything that really bothered them. That seemed to be okay with both of them, but the little one was a little more emotional than either of the other men in her life, and Grace wanted Tony to help toughen him up.

"It's that damned hippie shit. He needs a good swift kick in the ass. And what's with all this theater nonsense? I thought he would have outgrown that by now." Tony launched into a diatribe about the current state of affairs in the country, including his take on racism, communism, atheism, feminism, and any other -ism he could think of. They moved into the living room to watch the evening news, which only reinforced his opinion that the world was going to hell in a handbasket. Grace convinced Tony they should both keep an eye on Johnny. He was just the kind of kid they were talking about in the news, and she worried that someone might introduce him to marijuana. Tony's response was that "he's just enough of a smartass to try it!"

Johnny was friends with Nate Palmer in high school. They were both in the choir and both had played junior varsity basketball until Nate moved on to the varsity squad and Johnny moved over to the theater department. When the riots broke out in downtown Trenton, Nate warned his friend to stay the hell away.

Trenton became a war zone overnight. They brought in the National Guard. A handful of old Italian men in Chambersburg sat on their front steps with loaded shotguns, just dying for a chance to shoot the first black kid stupid enough to walk down their streets. Shops and businesses were burned and looted. Dozens of people were injured and over a hundred were arrested. One poor kid, a nineteen-year-old college student named Harlan B. Joseph, who was home on a break from his religious studies in Pennsylvania, got shot and died.

Curfews were imposed in the suburbs, and downtown became off-limits, even in broad daylight. Those who lived in the suburbs no longer thought of themselves as part of the Greater Trenton area, and even more businesses left the city over the next few years. Between the riots and assassinations, news of massacres in Vietnam, corrupt politicians, reverse discrimination, and the slow, steady rise of feminism, middle-aged white men felt like they were getting squeezed and started lashing out at the lazy shiftless hippies and their sexual revolution.

Johnny was a clean-cut high school kid who had grown a beard and long hair – originally to play a part in a school play, but he kept it even after the play was over. Deep down, Tony still loved his son, but there were times he couldn't stand to look at him. They argued loud and often about the politics and issues of the day. Tom sported a thick mustache and wore bell bottoms because they were in style, but he was the quintessential fraternity brother, doing well in school and headed for a career in business. He and his father both looked at Johnny like he was from another planet. Grace played peacemaker as much as she could, but their lives had all started to have separate schedules and priorities. It was hard to hold them together sometimes.

In the meantime, more than half of the Yackers Club had also moved out to the suburbs and their kids were having kids of their own. Luckily, they kept up the monthly meetings, and Grace would never miss one. She also made time to visit Marion, Bessie, and Carrie because she really valued their opinions – that, plus she never outgrew a sense of gratitude for the support they had given her when she needed it.

Tony could barely force himself to stay in touch with his brothers and sisters at all. He and Donny couldn't have a conversation longer than half an hour without driving each other nuts. His kid brother Johnny was too far away for anything more than a yearly fishing trip. Mary and her husband Red had split up, and she led a quiet church-based life, devoted to her son, Anthony. Jeanne and her son Eugene kept to themselves, too; as a single mother in a very difficult time, she was so afraid of giving people the wrong impression, she wouldn't even let her own brother in the house after sunset for fear of what the neighbors might think. Their youngest sister Fran was out in California and sent him letters he let Grace read and respond to for him.

Grace made sure Tony's brothers and sisters were invited for the Christmas holidays plus at least one summer picnic every year in their backyard. She did the same thing with the Yackers Club, as well as the neighborhood penny ante poker friends, and dragged Tony to every single event she could. The only event she didn't have to talk him into was their eldest son's college graduation. Tony took charge of that picnic like he was a man on a mission, and she was thrilled for his help. They had buckets full of beer and soft drinks, picnic tables covered in red and white checkered cloths, paper plates with plastic forks and knives, ketchup, mustard, relish, salads, rolls, chips, dips, pickles, onions, sliced tomatoes, corn on the cob, and a never-ending grill churning out hot dogs and hamburgers for what seemed like close to a hundred people.

Tommy's fraternity brothers, with their girlfriends, plus a few aunts, uncles, cousins, and friends from both sides of the family were all there. Tony had set up the badminton court at the far end of the yard and a croquet course in the middle. He was entertaining as many young coeds as he could while making sure the grill never stopped and the beer was always chilled. He was such a talented host that no one but Grace ever knew that Tommy actually left his own party for a little while to pick up a special guest. When he returned, they made an entrance so grand that everybody knew it.

Carole was a tall, beautiful brunette and the first woman Grace had ever seen on her son's arm looking as if she belonged there. She was, in fact, the first young woman he thought highly enough of to introduce to his parents. Over the course of that afternoon, Carole bit into a steaming ear of corn, shooting the hot liquid onto Grace's cheek; fell down playing croquet with Tony and got dirt all over her white shorts; spilled an iced tea on one of Tony's sisters; and charmed the living hell out of every single person at the picnic. She was a few years younger than Tom, and it was obvious they were falling in love.

Tommy landed a job managing the jewelry department at E.J. Korvettes on Broadway in Manhattan and became the first of his family to travel to his job by train. It was a grueling commute and the retail hours were long, but Grace could tell he liked the excitement of the city, even though he missed spending more time with Carole. She had taken him to meet her family, and now it appeared as if it was only a matter of time before they arranged to have their families meet each other. Grace truly liked her, and, more importantly, she knew that Tommy was happy, but she was nonetheless nervous when that long-awaited invitation actually came about.

Tony would never admit it, but he was kind of nervous, too. This girl came from more money than they had. It was obvious in the way she dressed and carried herself, not to mention the town she came from. Tom had told his parents that Carole's father was actually something of a genius, having graduated from college in his early teens and gone on to make a comfortable living with a big beautiful house in Medford and a wife with impeccable taste in food and décor.

Tony and Carole's father, Jim, hit it off immediately, and by the end of their first visit they were already close friends. Grace and Carole's mother were cordial and polite but a bit more formal than their spouses. Grace was a little intimidated by the size of the house, the furniture, the canapés and aperitifs; the way Carole and her mom spoke like Macy's and Wannamaker patrons left Grace feeling like a bargain basement shopper by comparison. Her own comfortable house seemed a bit shabby to her now, and she wondered if her little Tommy could keep up with these well-to-do people.

On the ride home, Tony was ebullient. "Did you see that silverware? I'll bet that cost a few bucks. Couldn't be a nicer guy, that Jim. Tommy's gonna have to make a pretty penny to keep up with her, huh? What do you think?"

Grace didn't know what to think. Her son was in love with a wonderful girl who just happened to be from a good family with a lot more money than his. She hoped she hadn't embarrassed him and was relieved that Tony and Carole's father had gotten along so well. She knew they would have to invite them over to their house next, since she also subscribed to Tony's practice of reciprocity. She just hoped there would be enough time to make a few changes to the household decorations and maybe learn a few new recipes. She didn't even know who to ask for help, until she found out that Eileen Schipske's mom was both highborn and British. Maybe that explained why her neighborhood friend was such a confident woman. Having received very little in the way of motherly advice, Grace was always eager for an older, worldlier woman's advice. Eileen warned her not to expect any revelations, having lived with the guilt of unmet expectations that thwarts the potential relationships of so many mothers and daughters.

High tea was not quite what she thought it would be, but the orange flavored scones were quite delicious. The real impact of the afternoon was that Grace finally realized she had a friend she could confide in. After observing how Eileen and her mother treated each other, with such formality and so much left unsaid, Grace opened up to Eileen in a way she had never imagined she would with another human being. Eileen listened in awe to the story of her life and held her friend tight, letting her cry for all she was worth. By the end of it, both of them were bawling their eyes out, and Grace learned everything between them would be reciprocal.

They talked late into the evening, letting their families fend for themselves, sharing triumphs and disappointments, worries and aspirations. Grace had always loved her family but had never known how good it could have been to have a sister. Eileen had always loved her family, too, but had never known how much it meant to be there for a friend.

"Are you sure you don't want to come back to Dunham's?" Eileen asked her with a devilish grin. "Can you imagine the trouble we could get into?"

"Not to mention all the money we could make selling second-rate dresses with a few new stitches!" Grace added with uncharacteristic deviousness. The two of them laughed until it hurt. It was nice to know where you came from didn't have to determine where you got to in life. It was even nicer to have a friend who understood that.

Grace never did go back to Dunham's. She liked her routine at the insurance company and the pay was decent. Tony would have been relieved if he had ever been consulted, but she spared him that task. She and Eileen got together often, sharing coffee and confidential conversations. They lifted each other up whenever one of them needed it but spent most of their time enjoying the company of a kindred spirit that allowed for both laughter and tears. Their friendship would last for many years.

Johnny graduated from high school and surprisingly decided to commute to Rider College like his older brother had. Grace and Tony thought he had the brains to do whatever he wanted, but they were pretty sure their little dreamer was going to run away and join a commune or talk his way into some far-flung adventure instead of following a more traditional path. Somehow, when it came right down to it, as he admitted only to his mom and no one else, Johnny was afraid to spread his wings too far, too fast, and needed the comforts of home a while longer. His grades had earned him a partial scholarship, and he worked full-time at the steel mill over the summer to earn the rest of what he needed to pay his way. He also found a part-time job at a tuxedo rental store near campus for extra spending money. He actually trimmed his hair and beard and even started wearing sport coats and nicer clothes. Grace and Tony weren't sure how it all happened, but maybe he would be okay, after all.

Tom and Carole had gotten engaged and found an apartment down in Cherry Hill, an hour farther south and not far from her parents. The retail hours on top of a New York commute were taking a toll on Tom, so he started looking for something closer to home. He found a great opportunity with the state Department of Transportation and started building a career. It would only be a matter of time before he and Carole started building a family, as well.

Even though it had snowed the night before, the April 8 wedding was spectacular. Carole was radiant. Tom was handsome. Johnny was the best man. Tony looked dapper in a tux Johnny had rented for him. Grace was simply elegant in a beautiful blue dress that matched the color of her eyes – eyes that glistened near the point of joyful tears throughout the entire ceremony and laughter filled with unbridled joy throughout the reception that followed. The Bankers, the Bullocks, and the Schipskes were there, and her aunts, uncles, and cousins, too. Tony's brothers and sisters joined the festivities, and all of Tom's college friends mixed and mingled with ease. Carole's family was warm and welcoming to all, and Jim and Tony looked as happy as the bride and groom. Even people who never drank much before found a reason to celebrate this union. The food and festivities were so warm and generous they filled all who attended with the promise of things to come.

CHAPTER TEN

WHEN CAROLE STARTED FURNISHING their apartment, she told Tom they needed corner cabinets for the dining room. Grace didn't know whether to laugh or cry when her son asked her if it made sense to buy them for a rental apartment. When Tony said it sounded reasonable enough to him and that he wanted to buy them as a housewarming gift, Grace's look alone was enough to freeze him where he stood. If she could have killed him and gotten away with it, she would have. Carole got the cabinets she thought would do for now, and Grace finally got the same ones, which she had wanted for years.

The newlyweds built a nice nest for themselves and furnished it tastefully. Even though they lived an hour south, they made a point of joining Grace and Tony for dinner often enough that they were never out of touch. Carole and Grace got along well from day one, but Grace secretly dreaded those occasions when she had to share the young couple with the in-laws. Carole's parents' house was just that much bigger, nicer, and more elegantly furnished than her own, and it made her feel a bit uncomfortable. They could not have been more genial hosts, but that did little to lessen Grace's discomfort. Tony going on and on about how wonderful they were for the whole ride home was enough to drive her quiet and introspective for days after every visit.

She tried to confide in her younger son, but Johnny took it too personally and actually made it seem worse, lecturing his mother about working class values and how the rich were responsible for the rise of the military industrial complex. She wondered what the hell they were teaching him in college. He seemed to be getting more radical every day. He was staying over in a friend's dorm room a couple nights a week and was going into Greenwich Village almost every weekend for concerts, rallies, and bar hopping. She was sure he was smoking marijuana but didn't really want to confront him about it.

They could still talk about almost anything, but the arguments between father and son grew in their intensity to the point where Tony actually threw him out of the house. It was more than he could take when his son insulted his brother Johnny for making a career out of the navy and announced he would have gone to Canada rather than Vietnam if his number had come up in the draft. That caused incredible tension between Grace and Tony. They were not on the same page, and both blamed each other for not being able to communicate with their own son anymore.

About a week went by before Tony swallowed his pride and called his son's best friend to find out where he was staying. Tony went and brought him home after having a long overdue heart-to-heart conversation, which both of them apparently needed from time to time. Grace took one look at Johnny when he came home and started cooking up a feast, convinced that he had stopped eating and lost too much weight in the week he had been gone. They all cried and hugged each other and started laying the groundwork for a more harmonious household. Johnny wasn't doing that well in school and explained it felt just like a factory to him. Tony tried to remind him what an actual factory felt like and warned him that he might end up working for

Fairless Steel the rest of his life if he wasn't careful with his choices. Grace looked for a middle ground and tried to convince her son to hang in there a little longer. He was growing more and more interested in music, the theater, and arts in general, so they suggested he pursue those things as a hobby on the side after he built a solid career as a teacher or maybe a lawyer.

When he went back to school for his second semester after a long winter break, Johnny seemed to have a better attitude, and things at home started getting back to normal. He and Tony kept the conversations civil, and Grace breathed a sigh of relief. Having played peacemaker all throughout that winter, she needed a break.

Luckily, her penny ante poker buddies had planned the perfect day trip. It was time for a little theatrical magic. They all took off a Wednesday from work and got tickets for a Broadway revival of *The Man of La Mancha*, starring Richard Kiley as Don Quixote. Grace, Eileen, Jackie, Madge, Peggy, and Ginny took the train into Penn Station for a long overdue matinee performance. They were already familiar with the story and the music, singing "The Impossible Dream" together on the train ride in, before they burst out in laughter at the sheer joy of having a day off together in the middle of the week, coupled with the excitement of heading into New York City.

The show was life-affirming. The sets, the costumes, the lighting, the orchestra, Cervantes's impossible characters, and Richard Kiley's breathtaking voice gave them chills, and, as Grace would admit to her son later when describing the awesome effect of the entire performance, it helped her understand how someone could choose a career devoted to the arts.

An early supper at Mama Leone's on West 48th Street did not disappoint. They laughed and drank wine together like the sisters they had become. Grace thought Concetta's meatballs were a little better than this, but she kept it to herself as a tender memory. The desserts were delicious, and the short walk back to Penn Station gave them an opportunity to shop for mementos of a day well spent in a fabulous city. New York was only an hour away, but the vast majority of their neighbors in suburban central New Jersey rarely ventured into what they called the asphalt jungle. The penny ante poker girls of Mercerville were not a timid bunch of ladies. When they wanted something, they went for it. Not a single one of them could ever have imagined asking their husband for permission. That was not in their vocabulary. The concept of feminism and the rising tide of young women burning their bras was a little confusing to them. They couldn't see what all the fuss was about.

As spring turned to summer, Tony got the garden going, Johnny started working full-time at the tuxedo rental store, Tom and Carole made lots of day trips to the Jersey Shore with friends and family, and Grace caught up with her aunts and cousins at family picnics. Skipper, the kid from next door who had moved down the block, had unfortunately never overcome the transition from adolescent to adult, and as an extremely overweight eighteen-year-old, he became a menacing presence around the neighborhood. He showed up on the screened-in back porch one morning and nearly scared Grace to death with his face pressed up against the kitchen window. He left peacefully when she told him he had scared her. He was committed to the state mental hospital about a week later after attacking his mother.

Johnny went to an outdoor rock festival in the Poconos, stepped on a broken wine bottle after losing his moccasins in the mud, and came home on crutches after a good Samaritan found him on the side of the road. His ride there had lost him in the madness of the festival because the medical tent had shuttled him off to a local hospital emergency room. One of the emergency room doctors cleaned and stitched the wound and sent him on his way after charging him five dollars for the crutches. He was lucky to make it home, but not lucky enough to escape more serious consequences.

When he tried to walk on the foot that should have healed in a few weeks, Johnny felt what seemed like electrical charges starting at the sole of his foot and running through his entire body. Tony decided to take him to a childhood friend, Dr. Louis Fares, who was like a god to him. They grew up in the same neighborhood, and Louis had gone on to become a doctor, surgeon, and eventually chief of surgery at St. Francis Hospital. He could do no wrong, so when he told Tony this was beyond his abilities to fix, Tony turned a whiter shade of pale. Luckily, he knew a specialist from Germany, Dr. Gerhardt Puchner, who was working in Princeton that summer, and this was right up his alley.

Johnny was eighteen, and though he never told his parents, he had to sign off on the possibility of an amputation in case the surgery was unsuccessful. Luckily, the surgery was a complete success, and the German doctor capped several neuromas which had been caused by tiny shards of glass left behind when the emergency room doctor stitched up his wound. They never thought of suing anyone, and Tony's insurance covered the full cost of the operation.

Johnny was lucky, but the doctor told him it was up to him if he wanted to walk again. He spent the next six months in a wheelchair, occasionally hobbling around on crutches with the assistance of his best friend, Tim, Jackie Bullock's son, who was a godsend. He dropped out of college, bought an old upright piano, and started teaching himself to play by ear. Over the next few months, he and Tim formed a plan to leave for California together, but they decided to keep it a secret.

Right about the time Johnny got back on his feet, the family that owned the tuxedo rental store where he had been working decided to expand. They were opening a new store in East Brunswick and asked him if he wanted to manage it. He knew the business, and the pay was good. He figured he could save up a lot of money in one year and then head out to California to make a living in music. He and Tim told other friends about it, but surprisingly they managed to keep it a secret from their parents for a long time.

Grace and Tony were both horribly disappointed that Johnny had dropped out of college, but when he started bringing home big paychecks and asked them to help him budget and save, they were impressed and figured maybe he had a career in business. He was making the company known at local high schools for prom season, and at local country clubs for their social calendar, and was doing everything he could think of to grow the business. It paid off. Even after lavish spending on weekends in New York and partying with his friends like there was no tomorrow, Johnny managed to save tens of thousands of dollars over the course of that year. He never lost sight of the goal of leaving for California and finally told his mom about his plans. Somehow Grace knew it was coming. She wasn't sure where he would end up, but she knew he had an adventurous spirit and needed to follow his heart. She would always be there for him and she would miss him terribly, but she, more than anyone else, understood.

Tony's heart was broken. First the kid who has all the potential in the world drops out of college. Next, he makes a small fortune renting tuxedos, but that's not enough for him, either. The family that owns the store even plans to open more stores and promises him a bigger piece of the pie to stay and become their regional manager, but he says he's had enough. The kid had it made, but now he's running off to California with a couple other hippie kids to do God-knows-what. Tony had grown up in a poor Italian family, served his country on an island in the Caribbean, married a nice Irish girl, gotten a steady job at a factory, and raised two healthy, intelligent kids. He worked three jobs to keep everybody well fed and clothed, and in every spare minute he got, he worked some more. Nothing in his life had prepared him to understand why his kid was going, and it tore him apart. He still had Tom and Carole nearby, but only Grace could help him hold it together when Johnny left home.

CHAPTER ELEVEN

THEY GOT A POSTCARD FROM Vero Beach, Florida, that read "having a blast – love, Johnny." Tony must have looked at it a dozen times before he threw it away in anger. They had driven south in a van and stopped to see an old neighborhood friend. John and Jackie Bullock's son Tim had left with another kid named Jim, whom Tony and Grace barely knew, and they were headed for God-knows-where, to do God-knows-what, for only-God-knew-how-long.

"Tony, he's got a little wanderlust. He'll come home again," Grace tried to reassure him, even though she wasn't all that sure, herself.

"Yeah, he'll come home when his money runs out." Tony was practical that way.

Their adventurous offspring sent postcards from New Orleans, Houston, Texas, and the Painted Desert within the Navajo Nation, before calling them once he reached the West Coast and rented an apartment on the beach in Santa Barbara, California.

"We're going to stay here a while. It's absolutely beautiful and close enough to the music scene in Los Angeles. We might head up the coast to San Francisco and check that out, but this is going to be our home base for now."

Johnny spoke as if he had a plan, but he couldn't explain it to his father's satisfaction. Tony could only stay on the phone with him a couple minutes before getting too emotional. He could not understand what the hell this kid was up to, but Grace had convinced him not to argue with his son, for fear it would only drive him further away, as if he could go any farther away than to some hippie town in Southern California.

The Vietnam War was winding down and the Watergate Scandal was heating up. There was oil on the beach in Santa Barbara, which the locals swore was the result of natural seepage. Billy Jean King defeated Bobby Riggs in the battle of the sexes, and Salvador Allende's popularly elected government in Chile was overthrown in a military coup led by Agosto Pinochet. Johnny filled his long letters home with the political and social leanings of his generation and only barely mentioned any personal experiences, let alone any revelation about his plans. Grace sent him care packages filled with food and clothing. Tony typed him a letter about the prospect of retiring some day and hinted how nice it would be for him to head back home.

Due in no small part to the empty nest they now shared, Grace and Tony rekindled the tenderness of their relationship. He drank less these days, tired of feeling tired. She ate less these days, determined to take better care of her health than her mother had. They went out with friends, to movies and dinner mostly, and even joined the Yackers for the occasional reunion. New neighbors had moved in next door, and both of them loved seeing young families with children start to populate their block. It made them feel young again, and their front porch became a gathering place for everyone around. Grace brought out snacks and pitchers of lemonade and Tony told his stories to a whole new audience. Kids did gymnastics on his lush green front lawn, and he shared the fruits of his garden with their parents.

They were already easing into another phase of their lives, when Johnny told them he was going to have someone come and pack up his piano to ship it out to California. They finally accepted that he wouldn't be coming back anytime soon. Surprisingly, the phone calls got more comfortable, and the letters were filled with warmth and good humor from coast to coast.

Johnny had finally learned enough songs to play a couple of small nightclubs in Southern California. He wasn't making much money, but he took odd jobs to supplement his income rather than completely deplete his savings. He was traveling all around the west coast, selling goods at craft fairs for a local cabinetmaker. He was painting a school building with a group of friends. He was working part time at a tobacco shop. He was laboring as a roofer, shoveling up after horses, building fences, and cleaning apartments. The way he explained it, it was all in the service of following his muse. So when he sent his mother recordings he had made with other musicians of the songs he had written, she cherished them and played the cassettes with pride at her monthly Yackers Club meetings.

Tony figured he had done everything he could for his youngest son, and the kid would just have to find his own way. Luckily, he enjoyed a closer relationship with Tommy, who came to him for advice on buying a home and a wide range of other household and domestic concerns. They weren't in any hurry, but it was obvious they were planning for a family, which delighted both sets of parents to no end.

It came completely out of left field when Johnny called to tell his folks he was getting married. Marlene was a California girl, eight years older than their son, raised a Seventh Day Adventist and a vegetarian. Tony wondered what the hell they had done to deserve this, and Grace was skeptical of this older woman stealing her baby.

Rather than join the circus for a beachfront hippie wedding, wherein the bride and groom both wore white linen and had flowers in their hair while guitarists played and sang, "Love the One You're With," Grace and Tony opted to pay the newlywed couple's plane fare for a visit back home where they could throw them a backyard reception and invite friends and family to give them a proper start together in their impractical matrimony.

Marlene was overwhelmed by all the attention. Tony said she looked like the actress Jill Clayburgh, but other than that he wasn't sure what to make of her. Johnny did seem to be in love with her, but she was either shy or reserved, both attributes her father-in-law had a hard time understanding. The young couple looked like they stepped off an album cover. They both had hair flowing down over their shoulders, and one of them had a full beard. They were both vegetarians, since she had converted him, but they both smoked cigarettes, since he had corrupted her. Grace found it hard to reconcile the health benefits of one with the recklessness of the other. She was absolutely sure they also smoked marijuana. All you had to do was look at them, but she really didn't want to know more than she could handle. Her new daughter-in-law was educated, had a good-paying steady job, loved Grace's son, and believed in his musical dreams. They were building a life together, for however long it would last, but as Grace admitted to her new daughter-in-law without intentionally trying to hurt her, she wasn't sure how long that would be.

The last girl Johnny had brought home was an art history major when he was at Rider College. She was unconventional, but so sweet and non-threatening. Grace would have given anything to see her again. Instead, she had to try and make room in her head and heart for Johnny's hippie wife. It was almost too much for her to bear.

As she listened to them go on about life on the west coast, she imagined the two of them getting older, so far away in California, smoking pot, selling macramé at craft fairs and getting so skinny she would hardly recognize them in the pictures they only managed to send back once a year during the holiday season, which they refused to call Christmas in a protest against the crass commercialism of it all. She had always wanted her youngest son to follow his dreams, but she had never imagined how far away that would take him. Now, here he was, sharing his life with an older woman, who spoke as if she knew him better than his own mother ever could have. Even though he had already been in California for a couple years, and even though they only spoke once a month at most, Grace had never felt a separation from him before. She wanted to like Marlene, but it was hard to let go of her youngest child. She blamed it on those damned vegetarian Adventists and planned to read whatever she could find out about them, just to make sure Johnny didn't get sucked into some kind of cult.

Surprisingly, Tony, who had had a much harder time with Johnny moving to California in the first place, accepted their new daughter-in-law much more easily than Grace did and even helped her put it in perspective.

"Grace, honey, they're in love. She's bat-shit crazy, but so is he. They're good kids, anyway, and they'll eventually figure it out. At least she has a steady job, and he'll find a way to make a living, even if the music thing doesn't work out for him. All we can do is give them a good send off now and then go visit them next year."

Tony had done a full one-eighty with regards to his youngest son. No matter how far apart their opinions and experiences in life took them, they had a bond that neither of them wanted to break.

By the time the newlyweds departed, Grace and Marlene had gone clothes shopping together and laughed like teenage girlfriends at the bargains they found. They developed a cautious kindness between them and got about as close as they could under the circumstances. Tony and John had had a heart-to-heart talk about a man's responsibilities, and both left satisfied that they understood each other as well as any father and son could.

The thank you letter John and Marlene sent to Grace and Tony made him happy and brought her to tears. She was relieved that her son was with someone so thoughtful. She only wished they lived close enough to get to know each other better, and she definitely looked forward to visiting the west coast someday.

As much as he wanted to leave the exciting world of U.S. Steel's security force behind, Tony was not going to retire anytime soon. He settled into a predictable routine punctuated by an occasional true emergency and tried to take as many late-night and overtime shifts as he could get. He had slowed down on the side jobs, as he and Grace no longer needed the extra cash quite as much as they had with two sons at home to feed and clothe. Grace no longer took odd jobs sewing, either, except for the occasional chance to help out an aunt or cousin for free. She was making steady money at the insurance company, and though she was a little bored, she and Tony were getting along well, and she had time for her neighborhood friends and family.

Just when they got used to having a little more leisure time, Tony and Grace both came home one week with paychecks that were not what they had come to expect. New Jersey started collecting income tax for the first time in 1976. That two and a half percent was supposed to help cover the rising costs of public education, but Tony was sure some of those bastards involved in opening the new

Meadowlands Sports Complex were stealing his two cents' worth of funding.

He was usually the happiest guy on Earth if he had an extra twenty dollars in his pocket after the bills were paid and the groceries were bought. Now his extra twenty was going to pay for public education when his kids had both already graduated, or worse yet, going into some governmental slush fund they could use to feed whichever crony had helped get them elected in the first place. The extra five bucks a week that Grace pitched in to help out the state was like adding insult to injury for both of them. They were venting their frustration over dinner one night with Tom and Carole, talking about New Jersey politics and wondering how young couples were going to cope with having to pay both state and federal taxes, when Tom had a strange response.

"Yeah, I agree. I don't think it's fair, especially for expectant grandparents like you two."

CHAPTER TWELVE

ONE DAY BEFORE HER FIFTY-FIRST birthday, Grace held her first grandchild in her arms. She would never even attempt to describe the joy she felt. "That's why people like you write songs," she told Johnny on the phone, when he called to wish her a happy birthday the next day.

Uncle Donny's daughter had actually had the first grandchild in the Calu family, but since she and her father were unfortunately estranged, Tony's grandson Matthew was welcomed by his side of the family as if he were the rightful heir to whatever they had to share. Carole's father had passed away the year before, or both grandfathers would have insisted on a parade. Grace would have taken the baby to the next Yackers Club meeting if she could have gotten away with it, but she contented herself to show pictures while she beamed with overwhelming contentment.

Another source of happiness was the fact that Tom and Carole bought a home in Ewing, a mere fifteen minutes away from Grace and Tony. It was a much easier commute to Tom's job, and the area offered them a bigger house than they could have afforded in her parents' old neighborhood. Matthew wasn't the only child they planned on having.

The days seemed to fly by, and they lived for the weekends, when Grace could bond with Carole and the baby while Tony helped Tom with any number of household chores and projects. Things were pretty idyllic on the home front. Unfortunately, life on the west coast wasn't going all that well for their younger son, and Grace's doubts about the durability of the marriage turned out to be well-founded. It looked like they weren't going to be able to wait for Tony's retirement to visit their artistic progeny. He needed help now, and they decided to use a little vacation time to do it in person.

Tony let Grace have the window seat so she could look out at the countryside as it passed far below. She loved the green pastures and geometrical shapes made by the intersection of farmland and freeways, not to mention the winding rivers, hills, and valleys, plus whole communities that looked like they belonged on a miniature train set, complete with church steeples, bridges, and big red barns. She asked the stewardess for a ginger ale to settle her nervous stomach. Tony lit another cigarette and read the inflight magazine. It took a long time to get from Newark, New Jersey, to Los Angeles, California. Then they had to sit on the tarmac and wait for the plane to let most of the passengers off before heading to Santa Barbara, so it was even longer.

Tommy had dropped them off at the airport and would pick them up when they returned in ten days. He half-jokingly complained about how long his babysitters were going to be gone and told them to wish his little brother all the best from him. He felt sorry for the kid, all the way out there in California, probably broke as well as broken up about his marriage falling apart. The two brothers had hardly spoken in the years since Johnny left, but Tommy asked his mom about his hippie kid brother all the time and kept tabs on him without letting anyone but his mom know how much he cared.

Johnny had borrowed a friend's car to pick them up at the airport. He looked even skinnier to Grace, who broke into tears as soon as she hugged him. They couldn't help but notice he had cut his long hair to a much more reasonable length.

"So, what prompted the haircut? Tired of being mistaken for a girl from behind?" Tony gave his son what he considered a little good-natured ribbing, as he hugged him, too.

"Actually, I just landed a job I'm pretty excited about," Johnny responded.

"And they let you keep the damned beard?" Tony couldn't help himself.

As they had agreed, Johnny took them to a modest hotel near the beach. He had moved in with a few friends since he and Marlene split up, and there wasn't any room for his parents to stay even if they wanted to, which they definitely did not.

They spent that first evening walking along the Santa Barbara harbor, enjoying the weather, the scenery, and each other's company, not to mention their first-ever Mexican meal together. La España had a terrific view of the beach and a bevy of attractive waitresses and waiters. Grace and Tony were both happy when Johnny ordered the steak fajitas. At least he was no longer a damned vegetarian. That phase hadn't lasted any longer than the marriage, even though he swore to them that it had broadened his palate and opened up his mind. So had Marlene, for that matter. They were still friends, and he hoped his mom and dad wouldn't mind going out to dinner with her later in the week. Tony said "of course" and that he was glad they could still remain friends. Grace kept her opinion to herself, knowing she didn't want to hurt her former daughter-in-law, but dying to say "I told you so" nonetheless. The fresh red snapper with rice and beans could not have tasted any better.

The walk back to the hotel was perfect, and they were tired enough for a good night's sleep. Tony would rent a car the next day, and they would meet Johnny at his new place around noon, so he could take them to visit the place that had just hired him. It was a Chicano community center called La Casa de la Raza, and apparently he was one of a few token Anglos on the staff. His high school Spanish had been good for something more than just ordering at La España.

The next morning, Tony was up early as usual. He left Grace sleeping and went for a walk to find a cup of coffee and a newspaper. Strangers on the street said "hello" as if he knew them and smiled without any apparent motive. At first it confused him, but it was so consistent in everyone he passed that he started to get the hang of it and eventually started greeting people before they even noticed him approaching. The waitress at the coffee shop smiled without expecting a tip. Even a cop said "hello" to him on his way back to the hotel.

"No wonder Johnny likes it here! These people are all nuts. They say hello without even knowing you and they're not even trying to pick your pocket or anything! You won't believe how friendly everybody is!"

He had brought Grace a warm cinnamon bun and a cup of coffee for breakfast, and she was convinced that everything tasted better in California. Johnny had a new job. They were on vacation in a beautiful place! Everything was right in the world!

When they pulled up to the address where their son now lived, both of them suspected everything was not quite right anymore. From the outside, the place was a dump: a battered old wooden house in severe need of paint, with weeds instead of a garden, on a street where it seemed every other house suffered from the same neglect. When Johnny took them inside, things went from bad to worse. The décor was left over from a yard sale, the sink was full of dirty dishes, and the place wreaked of stale smoke and incense. This was nothing like the pictures he had sent them of the way he and Marlene had lived, and Grace quickly regretted ever wishing them apart. What broke both his parents' hearts was when they climbed the stairs to see his garret of a room. A tattered sheet covered a shitty old mattress on the floor, next to an ashtray and a burning candle. There was no closet, just boxes full of clothes stacked beside his piano. Grace and Tony both took quick mental notes and measurements so they could get out of there in a hurry. It was all she could do to keep from crying as they got back in the car.

"Listen, kid. Why don't you go to work? We'll come see La Casa tomorrow, okay? Your mom's not feeling well – jet lag I'll bet. We're going to do a little shopping. Find a few things for your room, okay? Let us do it, please. Everything will be fine. We'll see you tomorrow morning."

They drove back to the hotel without saying a word. Then Tony went to the front desk and borrowed the local Yellow Pages. They knew what they had to do. As Grace started listing the items they needed, Tony drew a diagram of the space they had to work with. First thing they needed to find was a bedframe with a box spring and mattress, plus somebody to deliver it. There was room for a chest of drawers, and how about a god-damned rug? A pole lamp would be good, but they had better pick up an extension cord, because there was no outlet in that little alcove where the bed had to fit. Toiletries and cleaning supplies. The kid could use some new clothes, too. "Did you get a look at his shoes?"

They knew it was going to be a challenge, but they were determined to help him remember how he was supposed to live. They went about it with an incredible efficiency, borne of the life they had built together, without much help from friends or family who had troubles of their own to attend to. By the end of the day, their son had a new wardrobe in the trunk of their rental car, and all the furniture they could fit in his room would be delivered the following morning.

Grace and Tony showed up at eight in the morning with cleaning supplies in hand and demanded their son walk to town and come back with breakfast while they cleaned up his room in anticipation of the delivery truck coming before ten. By noon, their artist's attic had been converted into a clean and comfortable place to live. They turned it over to him and left to spend the rest of that day at the beach, knowing they had earned the time off.

By the time they met John and Marlene for dinner that night at an Italian place called the Chase Bar and Grill, their son had realized once again that there was no one in the world who would ever care for him as much as his parents did. The fact that he risked taking his father to an Italian place was not lost on Grace, who embraced Marlene like the long lost daughter she now felt had left too soon. The food and the wine were exceptional, and the owner, who knew the young couple, went out of her way to make her east coast guests feel welcome. She and her husband, the chef, were from the same town in Calabria as Tony's father, Frank, and their attention almost washed away the strains and stresses of the day.

Now that their son had a decent room to live in, they were happy to have a tour of the facility that had just hired him, and La Casa de la Raza did not disappoint. They met the old caretaker, who spoke no English, and yet Don Eugenio swore that he and Tony understood each other as if they were both from Durango. Tony's Italian was pretty close to Spanish as it came back to him from his childhood. Meanwhile, Grace admired the murals and the dancers rehearsing in a lovely little theater. Johnny had been hired to teach bilingual drama classes in grammar schools, and though his pay was a pittance, the people he was surrounded by were compassionate, creative, and devoted to the arts and their community. La Casa had a free clinic, a theater, a bar for concerts, classrooms, and practice rooms, a library, and a wonderful small restaurant for special events. Tony and Grace met everyone, and everyone was delighted to have their son on the team. They were left with a mixture of pride and relief that Johnny might know what he was doing after all.

The next day, Grace and Tony took Johnny to visit his Aunt Fran in Anaheim. Afterwards, Grace wished she hadn't convinced Marlene to join them, and they all wished they had gone to Disneyland instead.

When they drove up to the modest California ranch house, the first thing they noticed was a station wagon with a kayak strapped on top of it pulling out of the driveway. The driver, Tony's kid sister's red-headed husband, pretended not to see them and sped away as fast as he could. That should have tipped them off that there were problems, but it wouldn't have prepared them for how awkward things could get. Fran was so happy to see them, she cried while hugging her older brother. They settled down for iced tea, cookies, and a conversation like nothing any of them had ever had before.

Fran didn't want to burden them, but she was hanging onto the marriage by a thread and didn't have anyone else to talk to. She proceeded to tell them all the gory details of a sexually confused couple going in completely different directions with their lives and having real trouble understanding each other. Tony wanted to go hunt down the bastard who had just sped out of the driveway and drown him in the kayak he was surely paddling against the tide of all that was holy and decent in this world. Marlene, for some godforsaken reason, wanted to get deeper into the conversation, which Fran appreciated even though no one else did. She talked about different sexual behaviors from a clinical point of view while Grace and Johnny avoided eye contact with anyone in the group and got more embarrassed with each passing minute.

They were only there a couple of hours, but Grace admitted later the experience had aged her in a way that she couldn't explain. Tony left feeling frustrated that he couldn't help his sister but hopeful that she would take his advice and divorce this guy right away.

Grace decided not to invite Marlene to join them for the rest of the vacation. She gave up on the idea of helping the young couple reconcile and decided all she really wanted from the rest of her California visit was to enjoy the scenery. Tony could not agree more, and Johnny went along for the ride. They loved the views along the coast and through the mountain passes as they headed up to San Francisco. They managed to tour Hearst Castle, where Tony was beside himself. How could one man amass such a fortune and live such a lavish life? Johnny wasn't sure if his father was jealous or disgusted by such opulence. Grace thought it was beautiful but would not have wanted to clean it.

While Tony felt most at home on the beaches in Southern California, which reminded him of his time in Miami and the Caribbean during World War II, Grace felt most excited on the streets of San Francisco. It was like someone took all the best of New York City and added nice weather and incredible scenery. She posed like a geisha in Chinatown, chowed down on all kinds of seafood at

Fisherman's Wharf, and nearly melted into the magnificent views around the Golden Gate Bridge. Johnny had a musician friend who met them for a tour of the Muir woods, and Grace swore she could understand the songs the birds sang as if they had been waiting to share them secretly with her. The tall stately trees enlarged her connection to the world around her and left her smiling, speechless, honored just to be in their presence.

They drove back to Santa Barbara and spent a couple peaceful days enjoying the beach, dining out with Johnny after work both evenings. They put Marlene and Aunt Fran behind them, ignored the state of Johnny's humble abode when they first saw it, and concentrated on conversations about how wonderful La Casa de la Raza could be as a place for him to work while he continued to pursue the dream of making music for a living. They reminded him he could always come home if things didn't pan out here, but after seeing all that California had to offer, they didn't blame him for wanting to stay. They were in no hurry to leave.

CHAPTER THIRTEEN

WHEN GRACE SHOWED UP FOR WORK at the insurance company on Monday, she was greeted by a young, blonde, long-legged girl who couldn't have been more than twenty-two, wearing a short skirt and an expression of utter incompetence.

"Hi, what can I *do* you for?" she asked Grace casually, as if it were a clever greeting.

When Grace introduced herself, Kimberly almost swallowed her gum in excitement. She had heard all week that "Gracie will teach you this" and "Gracie will teach you that."

Gracie wasn't half as happy as Kimberly was to be on the same team. She made a beeline for the owner's office and closed the door behind her.

"'What can I *do* you for?' Is that what passes for a professional greeting? If you think I'm going to train this young girl to be my replacement, then you obviously don't think much of all the time and energy I've put into making sure your business runs the way a business should!" Grace stunned her boss with both barrels and was about to keep going, when he timidly interrupted.

"Gracie, who said anything about replacing you? Kimberly is my niece. She just graduated from Trenton State and needs a little office experience to help her land a job somewhere. I hired her part-time so she could learn the ropes." He went on to apologize if she misunderstood and tried to change the subject by asking her how the California trip was, but Grace was too wound up to slow down now.

"The trip was fine, but I've got something on my mind, and it's about time you showed me a little more appreciation."

She told him she would help him educate his niece, but she had a few conditions that had to be met. First, she was going to set her own hours from now on. She would still put in between twenty and thirty hours a week, as needed, but she would come and go as she pleased without having to punch a damned clock. She would hand him a schedule at the beginning of each week and that's what he would pay her for, period. Next, she wanted fifty cents more per hour. That was still a bargain after all these years, and he could either take it or leave it. Finally, she was done making his coffee, so his niece or one of the other girls had better learn how he liked it from now on. If her demands were acceptable, her next paycheck would reflect it, and if not, he could try to replace her with his niece. She didn't wait for his answer. She stormed back out of his office and slammed the door behind her.

Within days, Kimberly learned how to greet a customer properly. She started wearing skirts that didn't show off the color of her underwear, and her nail polish became clear, clean, and even, instead of hot pink, bedazzled, and smudged. Grace taught her how to file reports, how to answer the phone and take a message, and how to make her uncle's coffee. Grace knew what she did wasn't rocket science, but she took pride in doing it right.

In 1978, right after their grandson turned two, and around the same time Tony started to become a Reagan Democrat before the next election, they welcomed their granddaughter Dina into the family. Tony was happy she was healthy, but Grace was beside herself. She and Carole shared visions of spoiling her rotten with every pink, frilly, girly thing they could think of. Grace even bought a slew of books to read to her, determined to make sure her granddaughter grew up in a world where a woman was loved, respected, and afforded every opportunity. It wasn't the first time Grace had looked at books that way.

She had given a set of *Cherry Ames, Student Nurse* books to Tony's niece JoAnne that would turn out to be a major influence in her life, and she had given her own youngest son a book about South America that might explain some of his fascination with the Spanish language.

Grace was not a particular fan of Ronald Reagan like Tony was. He was okay as an actor, but she actually liked Jimmy Carter as president. He seemed like a decent human being, and she liked what was happening in the country with young people speaking their minds. Her trip to California had opened her up to things she had only read about before. When Jim Jones convinced nine hundred members of his cult to commit suicide in Guyana, Grace felt sorry for those poor lost souls and knew it was a spiritual crisis that drove lonely people to seek community so desperately that they would follow dangerous men like him. Tony, on the other hand, was convinced that every cult started in California led by libertine leftists that only Reagan could help rid the country of for good. They didn't talk about it much, but husband and wife saw the world around them very differently.

Grace started to dress a little differently now, too. She stopped wearing high heels every day and saved them for special occasions. She wasn't worried about being "shorty" anymore and felt more comfortable being true to herself. She bought a few loose-fitting blouses with paisley patterns and dresses adorned with spring flowers. She found contemporary pieces of jewelry in turquoise and jade that spoke to her and awakened a connection to Native American designs. She even stopped coloring her hair and let it go naturally gray. She was careful not to go overboard and stayed professional in her appearance at work, but there was something so free about her reflected in everything she cooked, ate, read, and wore, that Tony couldn't help but notice as he went in the opposite direction.

Having two grandchildren now, there was one thing they completely agreed on: weekends were meant for them. Both of them, having gone through the Depression as children, found comfort in knowing their family would always be well-fed. They bought an extra refrigerator and even a full-size freezer for the basement. They stocked both with everything imaginable and lined the basement stairway with canned goods. They filled a huge closet with paper goods, chips, and pretzels, and looked for more space to keep non-perishable items, in case they had an army to feed someday. Tom and Carole started coming over on Saturdays as if they were going shopping. Grace would hand them grocery bags and Tony would show them the specials they had found that week. The grandchildren grew up thinking this was how everyone lived.

As the kids grew older, Tony became the most entertaining person they would ever know. His ability to tell tall tales with heartfelt animation and lively sound effects kept them spellbound for hours. Tom, Carole, and even Grace just rested after serving the audience snacks. Tony took care of the rest. When a third child, Adam, showed up unexpectedly, two years after his sister and right on cue, the kids took over their grandparents lives, and neither of them would have had it any other way.

In the meantime, La Casa had turned out to be exactly what Johnny needed. He was teaching workshops in theater and songwriting in a variety of school settings. He was playing in local clubs and writing pieces for dance troupes and Chicano theater groups. He was recording with lots of local musicians and building a solid reputation in Southern California as a songwriter, background singer, and even a budding arranger. When La Casa hired him to be the opening act for a world famous jazz vibraphonist, Cal Tjader was so impressed with the young singer that he took him out on tour. Johnny ended up playing with guys who were thirty years older than he was and well established in the music world.

Chic Streetman taught him how to sing the blues and introduced him to Mississippi Charles Bevel. They took him with them to open for Taj Mahal, and he ended up rooming with the assistant producer for the Monterey Jazz Festival somewhere along the way. He met Dave Brubeck and Sarah Vaughan, and kissed Miles Davis' ring. He hung out and partied with Freddie Hubbard, and Etta said he could sing.

Grace hung onto every celebrity's name as if he were climbing the ladder. Tony just shook his head and worried, afraid that his son's life could shatter. He remembered his sister's dreams of a career in opera and never did trust the arts. How could a poor Italian kid from Trenton, New Jersey, ever make it big? Grace reminded him that Sinatra was from Hoboken, but Tony still couldn't quite imagine it happening for his son. When Johnny called to tell them he had been hired by Jane Fonda to run a songwriting program at her summer camp, neither one of them could contain their joy. Grace bought all of her workout tapes and told everyone that Johnny was working for her. Tony was quick to point out he hated what she had done in Vietnam, but she sure was one shrewd businesswoman, and one hell of an actor, too, just like her father. Even Tommy started telling his friends what was up with his long-lost brother.

Speaking of long-lost, it seemed like ages since Grace had gotten together with the girls from the neighborhood. She reached out to see how Eileen was doing, and her timing could not have been better. Eileen had a Saturday off, so they decided on a day trip to Smithville to browse in the crafts shops and have a nice lunch, with time to catch up on each other's increasingly fast-paced lives.

They both liked the way the other was dressed. It seemed that Eileen's recent Florida trip to visit her son Bill, who used to be in a band with Grace's son Johnny, had affected her in some similar ways. They loved each other's taste in jewelry and found new necklaces in a Smithville silver shop. It would have been hard to tell which appreciated the other more. These two had chosen to be sisters and had each missed each other a lot.

Over lunch, they started to talk about their sons' choice of partners, and each had a story or two to tell. Eileen had met Marlene briefly when the honeymooning couple first visited his parents.

"You knew it wouldn't last, Grace. I heard you say it under your breath."

"I wish I hadn't been right, but at least they managed to stay friends, and he really does seem to be doing pretty well these days," she offered.

It was a fair assessment.

"I think, if Bill ever leaves Diane, she'll hunt him down and kill him. He jumps whenever she snaps her fingers. I wish he would put her in her place," Eileen admitted without hesitation. She continued, "What is it about these young women who have to be in charge? Don't they know that men behave better when you let them think they have a choice?" Grace laughed so hard, her drink almost came through her nose.

"I've got a good one for you," Grace teed up a risqué story that only Eileen would appreciate and launched into the tale of Tony's sister Fran and her hopefully soon-to-be-ex-husband.

"Oh my God! I can just imagine Tony's face. And Marlene kept asking for more details?"

Grace nodded, unable to speak, and the two of them laughed uncontrollably.

"What did Johnny have to say?" Eileen wanted to know.

"Oh, we couldn't even look at each other, let alone speak." Grace had tears of laughter in her eyes.

"My mom had a cousin who used to dress up like a woman on holidays, but, then again, he's British." Eileen laughed out loud, as if that were the norm over there.

They collected themselves, enjoying scallops for lunch, and the conversation eventually got back to more familiar territory.

"So, you've got a third grandchild now. What's this one like?" Eileen asked with genuine curiosity, having already met the first two.

"Oh, this one's going to be a handful. Did I tell you they're putting in an in-ground pool?" Grace ventured into a subject she and Tone had fought about ever since he decided to pitch in for their backyard dream without asking her what she thought of it.

"Did Tony offer to be their lifeguard, too?" Eileen shook her head, commiserating with her sister over her husband's generosity to everyone but her. They both agreed, sadly, that was how good men behaved, and they toasted their good fortune, repeating in unison:

"Generous to a fault with everyone but their wives."

CHAPTER FOURTEEN

AT EIGHT YEARS OLD, MATT already saw himself as an Olympic swimmer. He held his head above the water with ease in order to listen to the cheering crowd that he imagined watching as he raced through the water well ahead of any competition. His little sister Dina had a keen sense of style. She would only use a towel that went well with her bathing suit and insisted on sandals to match. Their younger brother Adam was part fish, part commando on a raid. He darted in and out of the house, carrying soldiers, throwing balls, pointing an imaginary pistol at his grandmother, then laughing with pure joy as he fell into the pool, pretending to be hit by the shot she returned in kind.

Tom fired up the grill for the steaks his father brought. Grace and Carole cooked corn on the cob and assembled a fresh garden salad. Life couldn't get any better than a backyard barbecue and pool party. Grace and Tony never made it to the shore for any more than day trips that summer. They spent almost every weekend with the kids. If they weren't at the pool, the kids were over at their house. It was an idyllic time for all of them, but life around them wasn't standing still.

The woods where Tom and Johnny had played as kids in Mercerville had been plowed down to make room for commercial properties and another housing development. The road Grace crossed to get to work in the morning had become a bustling minor highway. Nobody went to downtown Trenton anymore. Businesses were all following their clients out to the suburbs. Quakerbridge Mall was in full swing, and towns like Lawrenceville and Princeton didn't seem as far away as they once had. Tom and Carole were talking about moving out of Ewing because the high school was starting to go downhill. It made sense to Tony, who wanted nothing but the best for his grandchildren, but it confused Grace. She felt like they were chopping away at their foundation and uprooting the family, right when they were starting to flourish where they were. She still had relatives in Trenton among the Yackers Club members, and it was getting harder to stay in touch. News from the old neighborhoods of her childhood read like a police blotter these days. Robberies and vandalism seemed far too common, and white flight was almost complete.

The government had bailed out Chrysler a few years back, and Lee Iacocca was now touting their success in television commercials. But U.S. Steel, where Tony worked, was in the middle of a long decay, with rumors that they were about to hand their security over to a private firm with a reputation for slashing benefits and getting rid of anyone who wouldn't accept a minimum-wage position. Tony's retirement couldn't come soon enough.

Tony was the one who smoked, but Grace was the one getting winded. She thought maybe it was just the summer, because the heat started getting to her like it never had before. Even when the fall came though, she was feeling so tired all the time that she decided to see her doctor about it. She had high blood pressure and she was overweight. He put her on some pills and suggested she exercise. She took the pills and made a half-hearted attempt to walk more than just the few blocks to work and back.

Just when she was starting to feel a little better, Johnny let her know that his life was falling apart again. He had produced a children's album with Jane Fonda that garnered him some minor critical acclaim, but it had been a complete commercial failure. He was feeling jaded in the record business, and his latest girlfriend had left him, too. He wasn't sure what he was going to do, and she had only one suggestion. She told him to come back home. He had given his dreams a valiant effort, but maybe it was time to get a normal job, find a girl, and settle down. He had a much better chance of making that happen back home with his family's support. He told her he'd think about it. She told him he wasn't getting any younger and neither was she.

Tony had gone back to drinking more lately, and he hated his job with a passion. He seemed angry at the whole world, as if it owed him a better life. Grace looked forward to the weekends, when they could spend time with the kids. Tony behaved himself better when they were around, because he knew Tom and Carole wouldn't let him see the kids if he didn't. They were the only thing that kept him going.

As much as she loved them with all her heart, the grandchildren weren't the only thing that kept Grace going. She needed her friends and family, plus a sense of communion with God. She hadn't read a good book in a long time and was watching soap operas to avoid looking at her own life's drama. She, too, was getting bored and angry with life, and she was mad at herself for allowing it to happen.

Johnny came back to New Jersey and sunk into his parent's couch. He was every bit a broken man, thirty years old, without a dime to his name. Overweight and nearly alcoholic, he smoked, womanized, and gambled, bitter at what he hadn't been able to achieve. He found part-time work at a friend's music store, where he made decent money and re-established local connections in the music business. He rented a room on the Jersey Shore from a bartender friend who had a house, and he crashed at other friends' apartments in New York City to divide his time and provide an escape from his parents' sympathy and embarrassment. He and Tony started to become drinking buddies, which did not amuse Grace, but she decided to bide her time and let her son figure out how to right his own sinking ship. As long as he didn't commit any crimes or cause them any undue heartache, there would be food on the table for him and a place he could still call home.

She was pleasantly surprised by how Tony treated him and how close they became. When Johnny cried about his failed marriage, Tony finally admitted to his son that he had also failed at one marriage before he met his match. Grace already knew that Tony had a wartime bride and got his "Dear Tony" letter when he was stationed overseas, but when she heard him tell Johnny all about it, she felt a strange sense of pride that the two of them had been so honest with each other from the start and that they had weathered all the rest of life's storms together so well over the past forty years. She hoped her son would be so lucky. She also hoped he would get his act together soon, since the last thing she needed was a retired husband and an unemployed musician son, both expecting her to cook and clean for them the rest of her life.

By the time Tony's retirement party came, Johnny had made a few modest improvements in his life. He was working more and drinking less, but still far from fully engaged in anything productive for a man of his age. Grace was losing her patience, while somehow Tony was finding his. At sixty-five, Tony was in fairly decent shape. He was slender, primarily due to the fact that his ulcer surgery years ago had taken away two thirds of his stomach. He still smoked and drank too much, but at least the bitterness about him had begun to fade as he managed to close a chapter on a career he had never wanted in the first place. His social security, pension, and benefits were substantial enough to provide for their needs, and his attitude was one of gratitude for having survived to see it through. He started spending time reading again and even began helping around the house.

Johnny was spending less time at his parents' house and had finally found a few good friends who were helping him rebuild along a better path. Grace gave up her job at the insurance company. She had been ready to leave for a while. She started spending more quality time with Tony and the grandchildren, allowing herself to be hopeful again. It was just too little and too late.

* * *

Her heart attack started in her left arm, and at first she thought it was just another bout of bursitis, but then she felt it crushing her chest and stealing what could have been her last breath. It was only Tony's presence of mind that got her to the hospital quickly enough to keep her alive. Tom and Johnny were both by her side that same night, and she was home surrounded by Carole, Matt, Dina, and Adam a few days later. The road to recovery would not be easy, but she wasn't leaving just yet.

CHAPTER FIFTEEN

"**IN THE NAME OF THE FATHER,** the Son, the Holy Spirit, and all the heavenly hosts, I send my prayers. God, it's me, Gracie. I'm sorry it's been so long since the last time I reached out to you, but you know I've never forgotten how to find you."

Grace began the conversation with her heavenly father the same way she had approached him since she was five years old. After her earthly father had proved too frail for a lengthy passage in this life, her maternal grandmother had taken it upon herself to teach her how to find comfort in the heart of the almighty. It was a lesson she practiced often and one she would never forget.

"Uncle Len told me you would never give us more than we can handle. I have to tell you, I almost laughed out loud when he said it. I didn't want to hurt his feelings, but you must think I'm a lot stronger than I am. The doctor said it was a heart attack and that sounds about right. I don't have the words to describe how painful it was, but thanks for seeing me through it. I guess you're not done with me yet. If it's okay with you, I'd like to start at the beginning one more time and see if talking it over leads me where I need to be."

This was how Grace always communed with her maker, by reviewing an honest account of her life in brief, up to the point where she now found herself. It was how she summoned all that she had ever learned and organized it to face the task at hand.

"I was born in Trenton, New Jersey, to a loving mother and a kind but fragile father. They provided for me the best they could and had the help of a large and caring family. We made it through the Great Depression by hard work and charity. We should never forget how lucky we were to have survived at all. My father died when I was young, and his mother looked after me while my mom tried to cope with her loss. She never really did get over him and lost her battle with blood pressure and depression when I was fifteen years old. Thanks to my aunts and uncles, I still had somewhere to belong. Aunt Bessie put a roof over my head and saw me through high school. Aunt Marion took me in when I was pregnant and alone. Her kindness probably saved my life when I lost the baby. Please be good to her and Uncle Len. Nobody deserves your blessings more than they do. Aunt Carrie and Uncle Jake were always good to me, too, and Aunt Myrtle did what she could, even though she had a lousy husband and too many kids to look after."

Grace sat at the kitchen table looking out at the backyard. She paused to watch a pair of blue jays gather sticks to build a nest. Tony had finally left her alone for what seemed like the first time in ages, and she was enjoying a quiet moment, starting to feel grateful for her lot in life.

"I was on my own for a short time, and it felt good to pay my own way, even if I didn't have a lot. When I met Tony, it was like something out of a fairy tale. He had this big, happy family, and his mom and dad treated me like I was someone special. Tony has always been good to me, even more today than ever. If I die before him, I hope you'll help him find someone who cooks Italian. He says my food is great, but I know he still misses what his mom could make.

"We have been blessed with two healthy sons and now three grandchildren. So, really, God, I have no right to complain about anything. Tommy is as steady as a rock, a good provider, husband, and father. I hope he learns how to be happy with what he's got. Right now, he's too busy chasing after more and more, but I guess we're all like that when the kids are young. Johnny is another story, and I think I may have screwed him up by encouraging him to follow his dreams so much. I should have listened to Tony a long time ago and convinced him to get a steady job first and keep his music on the side. I hope it's not too late for you to help him find his way. He's got a good heart, but he really needs a push in the right direction.

"So, back to Tony and the grandkids. I think they are actually perfect for each other. They bring out the tender, playful man I fell in love with, and he shows them the true joy of simply being alive. Okay, God, I guess you've helped me do it again. I am thankful for the birds that built a nest in my backyard. I am thankful for all the family and friends that you have placed in my life. I am thankful for the man with whom you have helped me build a life, and I am thankful for the children and grandchildren we share. I'll try to take a little better care of myself and hope you will let me stay around a while longer. Thanks for always being here when I need you. In the name of the Father, Son, Holy Spirit, and all the heavenly hosts, Amen!"

She heard Tony's car pull into the driveway and smiled at *His* good timing.

"Hey honey, is everything okay?" he asked with genuine concern before allowing himself to be reassured by her serene smile. Then he proceeded to unload enough groceries to feed a family of eight for the next month and a half. He delighted in showing her every single item as he put them away and telling her what an amazing bargain hunter he had become. "The kids are gonna love these ice pops. Look at all the flavors. Oh, don't forget, you're teaching me how to use the pressure cooker tonight. I want to learn how to make ham and cabbage. Is Johnny going to be home this weekend?"

Tony hid his concern about his wife's health behind a never-ending optimistic banter. He woke up early and did laundry, went shopping, then came back to clean the house. After a quick afternoon nap, he'd make dinner during the week, and both of them looked forward to lively Saturdays with the grandchildren followed by leisurely Sundays to read the newspaper and watch TV together.

The doctor wanted Grace to start getting some exercise, so Tony bought her a nice new pair of Rockport walking shoes. They looked so geriatric, old, and ugly that she hid them in the back of her closet and put on a pair of Nikes instead before heading out the door in an attempt to take a walk around the block. She planned to stop by and visit Jackie Bullock if she got too tired to make it all the way, but she overestimated her stamina by a long shot and found herself out of breath less than halfway there. Johnny drove by her on his way home and knew right away something was wrong. He quickly parked the car and ran to where she was resting, a little less than nonchalantly leaning on a row of bushes and standing unsteadily on the sidewalk. He knew her well enough not to challenge her pretense.

"Hey, Mom. That's enough for today. Let me walk you back home, so we can have lunch."

He took her by the arm and could feel her trembling. She made a valiant effort to hide how exhausted the fifty-yard walk had left her. She leaned up against her son, reluctantly, and they took what must have looked like a three-legged walk back home. She refused his help climbing the three steps up onto the front porch and flashed genuine anger at him when he tried to insist. Nobody was going to make her feel like an invalid, no matter how good their intentions were.

Over the next month, Grace built up her strength. She made it to Jackie Bullock's house for coffee, and after resting a while, she made it back home on her own two feet, even though Jackie had offered to give her a ride. She only managed to get out of the house a few hours a week, and she wasn't going to cut that short for anything.

Tony wasn't exactly the galloping gourmet, but he had mastered a couple of basic recipes, and luckily Carole cooked dinner once in a while for better flavor and variety. Johnny stopped by for lunch, bringing takeout foods they both enjoyed even though they both knew they were unhealthy as hell. The two of them had long talks about her health and his future, but since neither of them was doing much listening, they changed the subject and decided to enjoy each other's company instead. Grace told her son stories about her family, and Johnny told his mom tales about his time in California. They both left out the parts they were sure would have been too much for the other to bear, but gave each other enough of a picture to put flesh on the bones, so to speak.

Johnny could see the skinny young Grace, holding her mother's hand, standing in a breadline at the height of the Depression. Grace could see her young hippie son, hiking in the beautiful foothills of Santa Barbara without a care in the world. The son could see his mother as a young single woman, living on her own and eating mayonnaise and potato chip sandwiches because it was all she could afford. The mother could see her son temporarily turning into a vegetarian because he felt guilty for having eaten so many animals while he was growing up. Johnny could see his mother being welcomed into a boisterous and happy, Italian family. Grace could see her son, leaving his family behind, failing at a marriage, and feeling all alone in the world. Through the laughter, tears, and shared reflections, they got as close as any two people ever could. Neither thought they were anywhere near the end of their road together.

One mild winter morning, Tony and Grace joined Bob and Eileen for a drive out to Lancaster County to visit the Amish farms, taste the delicious fresh baked goods, and pick up a few new craft ideas to work on. They had an amazing time together that day, and Johnny watched his mother and father holding hands as they walked up the sidewalk toward the house. Grace even let Tony take her hand and help her up the front porch steps. They were both laughing when their son opened the door for them. Their smiles spoke years of tenderness and the appreciation of a day spent joyfully.

Johnny was hosting a songwriter's showcase that night when his father called to tell him to get to the hospital. He and his brother arrived at the same time. They were greeted by their father and Grace's Aunt Marion. They were all led into a small room by a priest who told them that Grace had passed. Their first reaction was anger – pure, raw, and confused. It was much too soon to lose someone they all still loved so much. But then, the touch of a father's hand, a brother's painful tears, and the sadness on the face of an aunt who had been with her all these years, slowly turned their pains to sorrow, knowing she would not share tomorrow. Her life had been an open book, a struggle from the start. No one they had ever known had given more of her heart.

CPSIA information can be obtained
at www.ICGtesting.com
Printed in the USA
LVHW091231110819
627231LV00001B/327/P